1/20

MIGRATING TO PRISON

MIGRATING TO PRISON

America's Obsession with
Locking Up Immigrants

CÉSAR CUAUHTÉMOC
GARCÍA HERNÁNDEZ

THE
NEW
PRESS

NEW YORK
LONDON

Published in the United States by The New Press, New York, 2019
Distributed by Two Rivers Distribution

ISBN 978-1-62097-420-9 (hc)
ISBN 978-1-62097-421-6 (ebook)
CIP data is available

The New Press publishes books that promote and enrich public discussion and understanding of the issues vital to our democracy and to a more equitable world. These books are made possible by the enthusiasm of our readers; the support of a committed group of donors, large and small; the collaboration of our many partners in the independent media and the not-for-profit sector; booksellers, who often hand-sell New Press books; librarians; and above all by our authors.

www.thenewpress.com

Composition by dix!
This book was set in Garamond Premier Pro

Printed in the United States of America

10 9 8 7 6 5 4 3 2 1

Para Jesús María García, que en paz descanse,
y Eufrocina H. García

I know that what I am asking is impossible. But in our time, as in every time, the impossible is the least that one can demand . . .

—James Baldwin

CONTENTS

MIGRATING TO PRISON

INTRODUCTION

By the time Diego Rivera Osorio was three years old he was already a veteran of immigration prisons. He had spent most of his life locked inside the Berks Family Residential Center, or "baby jail," as critics call the one-hundred-bed facility northwest of Philadelphia where Immigration and Customs Enforcement (ICE) confines mothers and their children. Two years earlier, Diego's mother, Wendy Osorio Martinez, had fled threats of kidnapping and assault in Honduras, bringing Diego with her to seek asylum in the United States. "We came here because the United States is safe. It has laws," Wendy said.[1] But on crossing the Mexican border in 2015, they were caught by Border Patrol agents and sent to the Berks facility.

An hour away, Judge Walter Durling heard the deportation cases of many Berks families in the York, Pennsylvania, immigration court. A former Marine and government lawyer, Judge Durling was no bleeding heart. He denied three-quarters of all asylum applications he decided, well above the 57 percent national average. Over a period of two years, Judge Durling saw Diego on his docket sheet several times, and even to him, Diego was a different story. Diego, the judge wrote in August 2017, "has gone from diapers to detention in his young life with no understanding or exposure to life beyond secure custody." In that time, Diego had won a special visa for children, but the federal government didn't relent, and it still tried to deport him. With the help of pro bono lawyers, he resisted long enough for a federal appeals court to take his side.[2] Wendy didn't have an easy time either. Her asylum application was turned down. Fearing return to Honduras, she continued asking courts to reconsider.

While the wheels of justice slowly turned, Diego and Wendy remained in Berks until, finally, Judge Durling ordered their release, noting that, in his short life, Diego had spent 650 days in jail "with no end in sight." That night, sitting inside a Mexican restaurant at a table so high he could barely reach the food, Diego ate the first meal outside Berks that he could remember. Now mother and child live with a relative in Houston, waiting for the courts to decide their fate.

Diego's situation is alarming, but it's not unique.

I grew up in South Texas, four hours south of San Antonio in the southeast corner of the state, where the Rio Grande meets the Gulf of Mexico. It's hot, poor, and overwhelmingly Mexican, and in the 1980s it was a hub for newly arrived migrants. In particular, Central Americans fleeing civil wars made their way to the Rio Grande Valley by the tens of thousands. Working with Congress, the Reagan administration responded with money, federal law enforcement officers, and immigration prisons. The Valley became an immigration battleground.

In the farmworker housing project where my family lived, Reagan administration directives were not distant policy debates. They were life-and-death developments about people we knew: relatives, friends, friends of friends. As a child, I experienced the rise of a security-focused immigration policy mostly through overhearing adult conversations. Sometimes it took the form of a *tío*, an uncle, sleeping on a couch as he rested on his way up north. Other times it was my parents worrying about whether my grandfather's English was good enough to get him across the border. In the days before passports were required to get into the United States, his U.S. citizenship didn't guarantee he could return.

By the time I was a newly minted lawyer, I thought I was

familiar with the region's role in the story of U.S. immigration, but it wasn't until I drove down Farm-to-Market Road 510 for the first time that I entered a part of the immigration-law world that I hadn't known existed.

Every year, thousands of mostly white retirees take the out-of-the-way two-lane FM 510 to the Laguna Atascosa National Wildlife Refuge to see the animals: the snow-white egrets, the redhead ducks, the bobcats, even the ocelot—recently hovering near extinction—making their homes in the thickets of native bamboo. At the same time, migrants unwillingly travel the same route. Forced onto buses emblazoned with the Department of Homeland Security's seal—an eagle clutching an olive branch in one talon and arrows in another—migrants peer out from behind dark windows and through metal bars. It's a prison on wheels delivering migrants to the Port Isabel Detention Center, a 1,200-bed facility tucked between the wildlife refuge, a crop-duster airport, and the salty edge of the Gulf of Mexico.

The wild beauty stops at the facility's guardhouse, where standard-issue prison architecture begins: chain-link fencing, concertina razor wire, layer after layer of security screenings, and steel doors. Inside, migrants are handed jumpsuits color-coded to reflect their security classification: yellow for people who present a low security risk, blue for medium, and red for high-risk migrants. From year to year or facility to facility, the colors change, but the rationale for them doesn't: there's no one here who doesn't present a risk. Walking through metal detectors, with the heavy doors clanking shut behind me, accompanied by a guard and constantly watched through surveillance cameras, even I—an attorney waiting to meet a client—seem to pose a risk.

After days or months there, the migrants are brought into a small, windowless room and ushered onto long benches. At the front of the room, a judge presides over dozens of hearings five days a week. When I made trips to Port Isabel to represent people who were locked up there, Judge Howard Achtsam ran things. Migrants called him El Diablo—The Devil—because he deported just about everyone who walked into his courtroom. These days El Diablo works out of a nearby immigration court, but things remain tough for the Port Isabel detainees. Adding to the misery of confinement, almost all have to make their case for staying in the United States without a lawyer. In civil immigration court, there is no right to a government-paid lawyer. If you have the money, you can hire one. If you don't, you're out of luck.

Gerardo Armijo was one of the few who did have a lawyer—my brother, who, along with our eldest brother, heads the law firm I've been part of since my days as a new lawyer. I have a lot in common with Jerry, as his friends call him. We were both raised in the Texas borderlands about an hour west of Port Isabel. We were born into a community that is almost entirely Mexican. We are both Spanish speakers whose families have traversed the border.

There we part ways. I was born in Texas; Jerry in Mexico. I'm a U.S. citizen; brought to the United States by his mother when he was just eight months old, Jerry is a permanent resident—the final rung before citizenship, but crucially a step below the citizen status I was born into. Despite that, the United States is in his heart. While I finished high school and went off to the Ivy League, Jerry joined the Army. While I studied in plush libraries, he walked the streets of Iraq.

Patrolling in a tank one day, Jerry lost several friends to a bomb explosion. He survived, but the attack took its toll. "I got back to the Valley, and I was messed up," he told me, his soft-spoken words revealing a soul torn between patriotism and trauma. When he returned to his South Texas home, the trauma proved too much for the Purple Heart veteran, and he turned to drugs. Jerry was convicted of possession and placed in a special state-run rehab program for veterans. The combination of drug treatment, job training, counseling, and lenient sentencing for crimes was meant to get vets back on their feet—a thank you of sorts for their military service—and Jerry was meeting all the program requirements. Then, one day, he suddenly stopped showing up. No one, not his family, his friends, not even his lawyer, knew where he was. It turned out that he had been arrested by ICE and sent to the Port Isabel Detention Center. No one had bothered to tell his lawyer or the judge overseeing the rehab program.

Cases like Jerry's highlight how far reaching immigration imprisonment has become. His military service proved his love for the United States, but to immigration law, it's the passport, not the heart, that matters. The direct link between Jerry's warzone trauma and his criminal activity makes him unusual, but not unique. No one is sure how many veterans have been thrown into immigration prisons because of crimes linked to his experiences in combat. War affects citizen and noncitizen soldiers alike. For migrants who join the military, though, combat-induced mistakes shred the hero status veterans return home to and turn them into what politicians—both Democrats and Republicans—like to call "criminal aliens." In this, Jerry is indistinguishable from many people detained across the immigration prison network: longtime residents of the United States convicted of a crime who end up inside an immigration prison, waiting while they fight the government's efforts to deport them.

The rules that determine who gets locked up and who doesn't are a legal labyrinth. Most immigration prisoners face government claims that they don't belong in the United States—civil proceedings in which civil infractions are determined and where the power of criminal law is never invoked. Under this system, people who do not have the federal government's permission to be in the United States can be detained. Near Mexico, Border Patrol agents walk the brushland of South Texas and the deserts of Arizona. In cities far from the border, ICE officers swoop into workplaces and knock on doors, waking people while it's still dark. They have legal authority to arrest anyone whom they suspect of being in the United States without the required documentation. Come here to work, but find yourself in the factory when ICE shows up, and you can be detained. Come here fleeing for your life and present yourself to a Border Patrol agent, like many of the families whose stories have dominated the news cycle under President Barack Obama in 2014 and again under President Donald Trump in 2018 and 2019, and you can wind up on the wrong side of the chain-link fencing and razor-tipped concertina wire.

Yet having permission to be here isn't necessarily a guarantee of freedom. Immigration officers can also arrest anyone who came here for a temporary stint with the government's permission, and then stayed. And they can arrest anyone like Jerry, whom immigration lawyers refer to as a lawful permanent resident but most everyone else calls a green-card holder. He has the right to live and work in the United States indefinitely—even to drive U.S. tanks in U.S. wars—until he crosses paths with the criminal justice system.

Arrest marks the beginning of a legal process that often takes years to complete. People caught by ICE and accused of clandestine entry can go before an immigration judge, as do permanent residents with their varied lives, their jobs, financial struggles, families, and traumas. People apprehended near the border who can't prove that they have been in the United States longer than two weeks can be summarily removed—a procedure known a expedited removal, which in the summer of 2019 Trump officials kicked into overdrive and applied to anyone caught anywhere in the United States. The one exception is for people who have fled persecution. U.S. law says anyone who is physically present in the country can tap the legal safe harbor of asylum to avoid persecution in their home country. In this case, a specialized asylum officer employed by the U.S. Citizenship and Immigration Services agency, one of the tentacles of the Department of Homeland Security, takes a first look, and migrants who show a credible fear of persecution get scheduled for an immigration judge's review.

Some migrants are freed, either through the luck of an enforcement officer's grace or by convincing an immigration judge that the public won't be imperiled and release won't result in no-shows for court dates. Others have to stay locked up because Congress has declared that some people are too dangerous to be allowed free while the immigration court process slowly chugs forward. Edafe Okporo, a gay student activist, fled his native Nigeria after homophobic thugs robbed and beat him. In a memoir written years later, he recalled a mob breaking down his door, angrily yelling about the need to cleanse the community with his blood. "The men gripped me by my wrist and dragged me out of my house, but I could not scream. I knew no one would help me because they were all on the same side." Fleeing to New York, he was immediately detained while his asylum case made its way through the immigration court system. "What had brought a man running for his dear life into a jail?" he asked. "I had a visa; I had never been to the States before," he explained. The answer is as simple as it is perplexing: immigration law treats asylum-seekers as worthy of confinement. By the time an immigration judge ordered his release, he had spent "2,422,000 minutes in the womb of immigration detention," he wrote.[3]

Where the power of civil law ends, the power of criminal law begins. In addition to civil confinement, migrants are locked up because the government says they committed a crime by coming to the United States. Back in 1929, Congress adopted two crimes about migration: illegal entry, which punishes those entering the United States without the federal government's permission; and illegal reentry, which punishes those doing that after having been deported. Both were largely ignored for most of a century. But since the George W. Bush years, they have come into fashion. These days, illegal entry and illegal reentry make up the crimes that federal prosecutors pursue most often. In fiscal year 2018 alone, 105,692 people were prosecuted for a federal immigration crime.[4] Defendants charged with these immigration offenses end up jailed while they wait for the courts to hear their cases more often than do defendants charged with any other federal crime. They are locked up more often than people accused of violence, and they're imprisoned more often than people suspected of the kind of white-collar crimes that might leave them with cash to disappear with.

To federal immigration agents, people like this are viewed as posing a danger, but to Cecilia Equihua they are just ordinary people like her father, Francisco. A divorced father of two, Francisco lived in Los Angeles but frequently drove to Las Vegas, where Cecilia and her sister lived with their mother. In late 2010, Francisco made what would be his final roundtrip drive, leaving Los Angeles early in the morning and heading back late that afternoon. When he was pulled over for a busted tail light, police officers noticed a decade-old deportation on his record. "My father was arrested in 1997," wrote his daughter Cecilia, at the time a law student and now an L.A. public defender. "He told me because of his financial struggles to support us, he made a terrible mistake—he let his garage be used as a meth lab." For that crime, Francisco served four years in prison. Despite thirty-seven years in the United States, Francisco was stripped of his green card and deported to Mexico. With his children and his life in the United States, he came back. He was caught, convicted of illegal reentry, and sentenced to two years in a federal prison in New Mexico before being deported again. Now he sells avocados in Mexico. To Cecilia, "he is being punished for the rest of his life, since he can never live in the U.S. with his family again. And my sister and I are being punished with him."[5]

Facing criminal charges, people accused of committing immigration crimes are housed in county jails, private prisons, and federal penitentiaries before they are even convicted. Eduardo José

Garza, a father of three in the Rio Grande Valley, recalls the experience of being moved from jail to jail after his arrest for illegal entry. First, he was in a privately owned and operated prison in Willacy County, about an hour's drive from his family. Then he was sent to Houston, and then Laredo, before eventually being deported to Mexico. Like Equihua, he soon recrossed the border to be with his family. When police pulled him over during a routine traffic stop, they arrested him for not having a driver's license. The local cops who booked him into jail contacted ICE, and instead of just deporting him, ICE turned him over to federal prosecutors, who went after Garza with criminal charges for illegal reentry. He remembers the humiliation of being brought to federal court. "They treat you really badly," he says. "They don't talk to you how they should, as a human being. They bring you chained up as if you were a criminal."[6] But, no matter how he views himself, he is a criminal because federal officials decided to bring the full weight of the criminal justice system against him.

Today, immigration imprisonment is the norm, yet in the United States, while confinement has long been a central feature of criminal proceedings, it has been an anomaly when it comes to immigration-law enforcement. For most of the nation's history, we did not lock up so many people for the act of migration. More often than not government agents turned a blind eye to migrants who flouted the law, either letting them into the United States or sending them back quickly and, in comparison to today, painlessly. If they committed a crime, they were expected to serve their sentence; afterward, they could return to their communities in the United States. In effect, immigration law and criminal law were separate, and citizenship played no role in whether people ended up behind bars.

Government statistics bear this out. Throughout the late nineteenth and twentieth centuries, few people were forcibly removed from the United States because of a conviction. During the nine

decades stretching from 1892 to 1984, federal immigration officials formally barred from the United States 633,918 people. Of
those, a mere 14,287 were treated that way because of criminal
activity. Likewise, officials deported 812,915 people from 1908 to
1980 but only 56,669 because of a criminal offense. For the most
part, government officials were more concerned that the poor
would end up on welfare or that people had failed to meet visa application requirements.[7] Meanwhile, federal prosecutors seldom
tapped the power of criminal law to target migrants. Though entering the United States without the federal government's permission was a crime for most of the twentieth century, prosecutors
rarely tried to convict people for doing this. In 1970, prosecutors
charged a mere 575 people with an immigration crime.[8] Even in
1993, they filed immigration crime charges in only 2,487 cases—
just 5 percent of cases pursued that year.[9]

Not surprisingly, few people were imprisoned because of their
immigration status. Reliable prison statistics going back decades
are hard to come by, but as recently as 1994 there were only
8,604 people locked up annually while they faced federal immigration crime charges. However, that number grew to 97,982
by 2013, a mammoth 1,039 percent jump.[10] Imprisonment rates
have similarly shifted for people actually convicted of a federal
immigration crime. In 1990, there were 1,728 convicted immigration offenders locked up on an average day, but in 2013 there
were 19,100.[11] In 1973, the Immigration and Naturalization
Service (INS) detained only 2,370 people every day, and in 1980
that number had grown to 4,062.[12] But by the last months of the
Obama administration, ICE held roughly 40,000 people daily, a
number that would soon rise under President Trump, surpassing
42,000 daily in 2018.

During the last thirty years, both the federal and state governments have increasingly tapped their powers to incarcerate
people for how they move across borders. As a result, the United

States has the world's largest immigrant detention system, in which upward of half a million people annually now spend time locked up because the government claims they violated immigration law. Even with record numbers of migrants locked up, less than six months into the Trump administration Congress increased funding for ICE detention and federal prosecutors charged with pursuing criminal convictions against migrants who came to the United States without the federal government's permission.

Despite the historically unprecedented scale of immigration imprisonment, its sheer scope is often overlooked in conversations about immigration and criminal justice, and when it is mentioned, advocates, journalists, and academics tend to split confinement into two types: civil immigration detention and punitive criminal incarceration. Supposedly, civil detention doesn't punish; criminal incarceration does. While accurate as a matter of formal law, this distinction is a farce on the ground. It fails to reflect the reality of immigration policing and the lived experience of migrants. Whatever the law says, the conduct that leads to immigration imprisonment and the conditions of confinement are largely identical across the civil/criminal divide. And no matter its formal label, immigration imprisonment often has a devastating effect on those detained, their families, and their communities.

As with its better-known policing cousin—mass incarceration as criminal punishment—the immigration imprisonment story emerges amid the racially coded debates of the mid-1980s, when legislators built the war on drugs on the threat ostensibly posed by people of color. Long before Donald Trump spilled off the pages of tabloids, politicians claimed migrants were responsible for a substantial amount of drug trafficking. From the White House to the pages of major newspapers and magazines, rumors spread of migrants dealing drug-induced death and decay across the urban landscape. More recently, inflated fears of Muslim terrorists boosted immigration imprisonment. In the immediate aftermath of the September 11, 2001, attacks, Muslims who were suspected of violating immigration law—and nothing more—were thrown into high-security wings of maximum-security federal prisons. Adding his own emphasis to this decades-long story, President Trump shifted the federal government's attention to gangs. Whoever has been in office, for three decades the president, Cabinet officials, and top advisors have claimed we must imprison our way to a functional immigration-law system.

With all the hysteria about drugs, terrorism, and gangs, it's no wonder that the vast majority of people locked inside immigration prisons are people of color. Not only does policing disproportionately focus on black and brown migrants, but immigration enforcement does too, despite the presence of plenty of Canadian and European migrants who are also violating immigration law. "Historically we have evidence of more terrorists coming across our northern Canadian border than our southern border," Asa Hutchinson, a top DHS official under President George W. Bush, said in 2007 as the agency was furiously recruiting Spanish-speaking Border Patrol officers. How should the gargantuan department he helped lead respond to the northern threat? "The best border security on the northern border is the grandmother who has lived in her house on the border for seventy years. She sits in her home and watches the border and calls border patrol when she sees something suspicious," Hutchinson explained.[13] To the north, we rely on grandmothers in their living rooms. To the south we rely on prisons, agents, and walls.

Spurred by, or taking advantage of, racialized fears of lawlessness, those on the political right view migrants, especially noncitizens with a criminal record, as national security risks and threats to the rule of law. They are "criminals," former Republican Speaker of the House John Boehner said in 2013. On his first visit to the southern border as attorney general, Jeff Sessions instructed federal prosecutors nationwide to prioritize immigration crime cases. "Criminal aliens and the coyotes and document forgers seek to overthrow our system of lawful immigration," he told a group of assembled Border Patrol agents in Nogales, Arizona. "It is here, on this sliver of land, where we first take our stand against this filth." At the same time, many advocates keep migrants with criminal records at arm's length out of concern that association with the most unsympathetic members of immigrant communities might tarnish broader immigration reform efforts. Sometimes, silence can weigh as heavily as the crudest words.

Despite the common refrain that immigration law is "broken," immigration imprisonment is a sign that the United States immigration policy is working exactly as designed. The system hasn't malfunctioned. It was intended to punish, stigmatize, and marginalize—all for political and financial gain. Politicians get elected, local governments receive revenue, corporations profit, and white racists find comfort against the prevailing winds of change that bring different languages, different people, and new challenges to old communities. That is exactly what is happening.

Prisons mark the people locked up as outcasts. The coiled razor wire stretched in layers around the perimeter suggests that they are dangerous, and if they are dangerous then good riddance. Prison segregates migrants physically and in the public's imagination. They can be ignored, forgotten, or remembered only as the unknown threat that requires guards, cameras, and steel doors. At the same time, their unseen existence is used as proof that the threat is real. Erased of individuality, they become justification for strong-armed policing tactics and are flagged as evidence that elected officials care about the innocent public.

Immigration prisons are also surrounded in secrecy. Whatever happens on the inside stays on the inside—or at least that is

what the authorities intend. Confined in Arizona's Eloy Detention Center for 444 days, poet Alexandra La Golosa wrote, "In
Eloy we have dates instead of names. / Nobody asks while meeting
of your name— / They ask 'how much' and 'when.'" Their treatment, she added, was akin to "animals in chain." [14] Some migrants
talk about their time inside the "perrera"—the dog pound—
because they were locked inside large chain-link-fence enclosures
within Border Patrol stations. "When we arrived at la perrera,"
one woman said, "[my son] was taken away from me again." [15] Pe-
diatricians and psychologists say children should never be imprisoned, but federal officials say they have only two options: take kids
from their parents and lock them up with other kids, or imprison
families together. In today's topsy-turvy world, family detention is
offered as the humanitarian response to family separation.

Meanwhile, the safety of imprisoned migrants is hardly guaranteed. Sexual assaults are not uncommon. Consider Levian
Pacheco, a "youth care worker" in a Phoenix immigration prison.
He worked for Southwest Key, the nonprofit that operates the
largest number of facilities for the Office of Refugee Resettlement, the agency responsible for holding young people who are
no longer with their parents. After sexually abusing seven boys,
Pacheco was caught, convicted, and sentenced to nineteen years in
prison. Now he's incarcerated, and the boys he abused are forced
to live with their trauma.

Life is by no means sacred inside immigration prisons. Kamyar
Samimi was a young man when he arrived in the United States in
1976. Three years later, he became a permanent resident. Almost
thirty years after that, in 2005, he was convicted of simple possession of cocaine. The judge ordered him to do some community
service, but Samimi didn't get any jail time. His troubles might
have ended there. He went back to his ordinary life in suburban
Denver. But twelve years after his conviction, ICE agents arrived
at his home. They arrested him and took him down to a nearby

privately owned and operated detention center in Aurora, the city infamous for the 2012 shooting where James Holmes opened fire inside a movie theater and took twelve lives. Aurora would also be where Samimi's life ended. He died in ICE's custody. He "fell ill" and died of cardiac arrest, ICE said.[16] Some, including a local congressman, remained unconvinced; they wanted to know whether lousy medical care was to blame.[17] An internal review released a year later revealed that, despite his complaints of feeling ill, nurses checked his vital signs half as often as a doctor demanded and gave him less than half the medicine ordered.[18]

Samimi's death reminds us that "prisoners are persons most of us would rather not think about," as Supreme Court Justice William Brennan wrote in a 1987 case. "Banished from everyday sight, they exist in a shadow world that only dimly enters our awareness."[19]

Financial incentives push toward ever-growing incarceration. In immigration enforcement, private prisons have an outsized presence. Sixty-five percent of ICE detainees are held in private facilities.[20] Every year, private prison corporations make hundreds of millions of dollars off immigration imprisonment. "You sell [prisons] just like you were selling cars, or real estate, or hamburgers," private prison pioneer Tom Beasley said.[21] To entice customers with cheap prices, inside some prisons migrants are put to work for $1 per day. Whether it's voluntary, as prison officials claim, or forced labor, as many migrants say, it's certainly profitable to pay cooks and cleaners well below the minimum wage.

Like farmers and consumers hungry for cheap food, this is a story of symbiosis. But the relationship private prisons have with the federal government isn't one of an opportunistic industry meeting the needs of a willing customer. The private prison industry grew up alongside immigration imprisonment. Their modern histories began to expand jointly under the Reagan administration when entrepreneurial prison executives and investors convinced ICE's predecessor, the INS, that it could quickly take custody of an ever-changing number of migrants. Since then, that has remained the private prison industry's tune, and the federal government has become dependent on its supply of guards and steel doors.

Just like money matters, votes do too. In some places, immigration prisons are an economic lifeline. Across the United States, local governments have gotten into the business of immigration imprisonment by building new jails or enlarging existing facilities in the hope that the federal government will pay the bills. Migrants are turned into commodities—their bodies valued for the revenue stream they promise. Facing the possibility of an immigration prison shutdown, the mayor of a small South Texas town heavily dependent on prison jobs didn't mince words: "If we lose our prisoners, the income comes down. . . . We need everybody to be employed. We need those prisoners." Roughly 6 percent of counties nationwide contract with ICE to hold migrants.[22] Others use space in their county jails to house the U.S. Marshals Service's immigration prisoners. Whichever agency sends the prisoners, the counties take the federal government's money all the same. With that, they hire guards and pay for construction—more jobs for local workers, more votes for local politicians.

Instead of continuing along this path, the United States must rethink its approach to migrants. Toddlers like Diego can't be blamed for coming here in violation of federal law. No one asked for his opinion. But it's equally true that others do have a choice. After he was deported, Francisco Equihua decided he would flout federal laws yet again so that he could be with his daughters. "My job is to be here for you guys," he told his daughter Cecilia. It's a noble goal, but it doesn't erase his crime. His transgression is clear, but to his kids he's still just dad.

Migrants are just people. They are fallible, imperfect human beings. Their passports might differ from U.S. citizens', but the skeletons in their closets don't. Immigration law needs to accept that migrants are no better and no worse than U.S. citizens. The wife of Edgar Baltazar García, a long-time Texas resident and veteran thrown into an immigration prison pulled the veil off her family's two-handed treatment: "He's brave enough to come and serve this country, and for him to be detained, it's not right. There are a lot of other people out here who are U.S. citizens and they don't even have the bravery he does to serve our country," Jennifer García told reporters while sitting in my family's law firm.[23] She might have added that imprisoning people because they violate immigration law raises the dust of the racially charged era in which the immigration prison legal infrastructure was built.

This book takes a hard look at the U.S. immigration prison system's origins, how it currently operates, and why. The use of confinement to target migrants was dreamed up at very specific historical moments, and that history matters. It tells the story of fears of decades past refracted through the prism of the United States' troubled race and class relations. It helps explain why we now do what we do, and it hints at how to unravel the vast immigration prison regime. So how did we go from effectively abolishing immigration imprisonment during the 1950s and 1960s to today's pattern of locking up half a million people annually? To understand that dramatic shift, we have to step back to the late 1800s, when the federal government became heavily involved in immigration law for the first time.

Part I

THEN

1

LAYING THE GROUNDWORK

For the first one hundred years of the nation's history, the federal government was not heavily involved in immigration law. The only mention of migration in the U.S. Constitution comes in the Migration Clause, a fifty-four-word provision that guaranteed slavery would continue at least until 1808. During that same period, the first Congress in the nation's history adopted the Naturalization Act of 1790, which extended citizenship rights to "free White persons" who met a two-year residency requirement and possessed "good character." Adopting a variety of strategies, states, counties, and towns regulated movement across borders. Sometimes they focused on the external borders of the United States. Mostly they didn't. In those days, borders between states were at least as important as borders between countries.

Some states targeted people convicted of certain crimes. In 1787, for example, Georgia barred any felon from setting foot in its territory. Rhode Island targeted criminals from other states; Connecticut focused on those coming from abroad.[1] In 1837, Massachusetts began charging shipmasters a tax on some migrants brought to its ports. After the Supreme Court invalidated that fee in a decision called the *Passenger Cases*, the state started demanding that shipmasters post bond for all incoming migrants.[2] Meanwhile, several states targeted movement by black people. Some states that banned slavery made it difficult for formerly enslaved people to move in, fearing that slave owners would free old and economically unproductive slaves. Slave states didn't want free blacks either, fearing the bad example their freedom would set for enslaved blacks.[3] Some states expelled unwanted newcomers, some imprisoned them—others threatened death.

In the Civil War's aftermath, when citizenship was extended to former slaves under the Fourteenth Amendment, focus turned westward. For decades, Chinese migrants had worked menial jobs like laying railroad tracks and operating laundries. Estimates vary on how many Chinese migrants came to the United States during the mid-1800s; some research suggests as many as 300,000 Chinese, mostly men, moved to the United States between 1850 and 1882, the vast majority to California. California's economy became so reliant on Chinese laborers that in 1852 the governor pitched the idea of giving Chinese migrants land in the hope that more would be convinced to come.[4] The governor's idea didn't become reality, but Chinese communities throughout California did. By the mid-1850s, 12 percent of San Francisco's population was Chinese. Within a few years, San Francisco's Chinatown covered fifteen square blocks.[5]

Political tides turn quickly. The open-armed embrace of Chinese migrants proved short-lived. In the decades that followed the Civil War, the Chinese became the picture of undesirability, exhibiting the enduring power of racism brewed in a nativist political cauldron. Illustrating the sharp turn of events, white Californians led the anti-Chinese fervor. In 1879, for example, Californians voted on whether to encourage additional Chinese migration. Almost 900 votes were cast in favor. Over 150,000 people voted against. The next year, San Francisco's Board of Health declared Chinatown a public nuisance.[6] Meanwhile, the state legislature consistently adopted anti-Chinese measures throughout the 1850s and 1860s.[7]

Despite successful efforts to make life difficult for Chinese migrants within California, anti-Chinese advocates were unsatisfied by the slow and inconsistent pace of state-level tactics. They wanted to make life difficult for Chinese migrants in one sweep. The only way to accomplish this was through federal action. For this reason, they turned their focus to Congress. By 1862 they began notching a series of legislative wins. That year, Congress banned migration by Chinese indentured servants—"coolies," in the day's vocabulary. In 1875, Congress banned entry of prostitutes, a thinly veiled attempt to keep out Chinese women. Anti-Chinese lobbying in Congress culminated in the Chinese Exclusion Act of 1882—the only federal law ever to explicitly ban a national group by name. As a result, Chinese laborers could no longer come to the United States. Less than ten years later, in 1891, Congress again changed immigration laws. This time it excluded people who had committed a "crime involving moral turpitude," an intentionally vague concept that is deployed to this day and "refers generally to conduct that is inherently base, vile, or depraved, contrary to the rules of morality and the duties owed between man and man, either one's fellow man or society in general." Spurred by increasing hostility toward almost all Asian migrants, exclusion was extended to the "Asiatic Barred Zone" in a series of laws enacted between 1917 and 1934.[8]

With federal immigration law growing year after year, government officials were suddenly tasked with distinguishing between desirable migrants and undesirable migrants. Who, for example, is a prostitute? Who is an excludable Chinese laborer and who is a Chinese merchant, who is allowed to enter? Who has committed a crime involving moral turpitude? A quick once-over isn't enough to identify who fits into one category or another. The stark categorization of human beings, with all the messy, multifaceted nature of life, always fails. In one case, a divinity student was allowed to enter as a student but was removed once he started preaching—he had become a laborer, immigration officials said, and a court agreed. In another, a merchant became a laborer when he turned to selling fruits in a Los Angeles market after his grocery store failed.[9]

Government officials needed some way to figure out who was to be kept out of the United States and who could come in. Imprisonment provided the on-the-ground solution. Once migrants stepped foot on dry land, they had entered the United States. To the government, this was a problem. At the time, the Constitution protected people inside the country more than people who hadn't entered. Intent on vetting people arriving on steamships, government officials forced transoceanic companies to keep passengers on board until they'd decided whether a person was fit to enter the country. Anything else would be to allow migrants to enter before government officials had decided if they should be kept out. Second thoughts would require an attempt to locate and deport a migrant—a tough law enforcement task in the 1800s that was compounded by the fact that Congress didn't even enact the federal government's first full-fledged deportation law until 1891. That year, Congress granted immigration officials the power to deport anyone who had entered in the previous twelve months but should have been excluded.[10]

With the federal government's demand that ships keep passengers on board, immigration imprisonment had begun, and it started in the hands of private corporations. Not surprisingly, the shipping companies were not pleased about this requirement. They were in the business of moving people across oceans, not housing them harborside. Every day that a migrant sat on a ship was an inconvenience and expense. Passengers needed food, and the ship was stuck in port. Soon the companies and the government agreed on an alternative: the companies would provide onshore housing nearby. Steamship companies were obviously happy. They could now quickly offload passengers and cargo and send the ship back to sea. But doesn't this mean that migrants were being allowed to enter the United States before government officials had a chance to decide whether they should be turned around?

The practical answer is clear—the land around a harbor is definitely part of the United States—but the law quickly muddled the practical reality. In 1891, Congress adopted a legal concept that people could enter the country physically without entering the country legally. This twist of logic, known as the "entry fiction," meant that steamship passengers could be allowed off the boat without benefiting from the higher hurdle that government officials have to climb to deport someone rather than exclude them. For the government, this arrangement had a second advantage. They didn't have to spend time or money locating people who had arrived from overseas. Officials could simply go down to the company-owned confinement facility.

Thanks to the entry fiction, the immigration detention center became an in-between space in law. It was neither outside nor inside the United States. Whether in California or New York, there was never doubt that on-shore detention sites were physically within the territorial boundaries of the United States. The entry fiction is no doubt a quirky legal doctrine: a person can be inside the United States as a matter of geography and outside it as a matter of law. But it also served to wedge open a broader space within the law that allowed early immigration detention centers to operate with minimal oversight and to blur traditional legal boundaries.

Soon conditions inside early immigration prisons were atrocious. "The air is impure, the place is crowded," wrote one visitor to a San Francisco "Chinese jail," as the dockside facilities were often described. "I have visited quite a few jails and State prisons in this country, but have never seen any place half so bad," he added.[11] Another account goes into more detail: "The Shed—rightly so-called—is a cheap, two-story wooden building, at the end of a wharf, built out over the water where the odors of sewage and bilge are most offensive; unclean, at times overrun with vermin, and often inadequate to the numbers to be detained. The food provided was poor and the conditions even more unsanitary than the police cells of the city."[12] With up to two hundred people jammed into a one-hundred-foot building, an inspector for the Department of Commerce and Labor called the two-story warehouse leased by the Pacific Mail Steamship Company a "death trap."[13] Even the federal government's commissioner of immigration was said to have found the facilities too dirty for comfort.[14]

While on a minuscule scale compared to today's immigration prison practices, there are uncanny parallels. The migrants locked in these unsanitary, haphazard sheds technically had not been charged with a crime. They were just waiting to find out whether they could enter the United States legally as well as physically. But it sure looked and felt like prison. Sociologist Mary Roberts Coolidge, who wrote about the Pacific Mail shed in San Francisco while it was still in use, claimed that detainees were "all under the guard of ordinary police."[15] A former detainee said, "One may look to the right and to the left and see only bunks and benches. 'You stay here, you stay here,' is all they say. Here you are cramped and doomed never to stretch."[16] It is easy to see how migrants might have missed the distinction between prison and temporary detention tied to immigration vetting, because the sheds were often modeled on prisons. The vice president of one transportation company "successfully argued that the new detention quarters 'would have to be heavily stockaded and guarded . . . built and erected as a prison."[17] Completing the erosion of an already weak distinction between prison and temporary detention, sometimes migrants were confined in traditional county jails.[18]

With time, reformers sympathetic to Chinese migrants got wind of the atrocious and punitive state of detention. Their proposal was to take steamship companies out of the detention business. Instead, the government would run immigration detention—an "immigration depot" in New York harbor, as one congressional committee recommended in 1889.[19] Removing profit-driven transportation companies, they hoped, would eliminate penny-pinching and improve the treatment migrants received. Two years later, Congress responded. For the first time, federal law explicitly authorized immigration imprisonment, and responding to these congressional directives, federal immigration authorities quickly launched a prison network and boosted their capacity to hold people. On the East Coast, for instance, Ellis Island opened on January 1, 1892, serving dual roles as a point of disembarkation and one of detention. Working under the direction of the newly created position of superintendent of immigration, federal officers were required to inspect migrants arriving by sea. If they could not conduct the inspection on board the ship, officers could "order a temporary removal of such aliens for examination at a designated time and place, and then and there detain them until a thorough inspection is made."[20]

Immigration imprisonment had now been added to the nation's immigration-law infrastructure. Two years later, Congress revisited its newfound interest. This time it stripped inspection officers of discretion to detain. They were now required to detain anyone not "clearly and beyond doubt entitled to admission."[21]

Like its East Coast counterpart at Ellis Island, immigration imprisonment in California centered on an island just offshore a thriving urban area: Angel Island in San Francisco Bay. The passengers arriving on steamships in San Francisco tended to come from Asia. In the words of Hubert Howe Bancroft, the prominent nineteenth-century Californian whose name still adorns the University of California's library, these people were "in every sense, aliens. The color of their skins, the repulsiveness of their features, their under-size of figure, their incomprehensible language,

strange customs, and heathen religion" combined to make them a
"detested race."[22] Given this attitude by the era's civic leaders, it is
no surprise that they received a hostile reception. Imprisonment
was a central feature. From 1910 to 1940, federal officials used
Angel Island as an immigration holding facility. No comprehen-
sive figures exist about how many people were forced to stay there.
The best study indicates roughly thirty thousand people were confined on the island from 1913 to 1919. About two-thirds of those
were the Chinese who were famously targeted by state and federal
laws going back to the 1870s, but Japanese and non-Asian immigrants were also kept there.[23]

In 1913, three years after the Angel Island detention facility
opened, 38 percent of all people arriving in San Francisco were
held. Excluding U.S. citizens arriving in San Francisco, 60 percent
of arriving migrants were sent to Angel Island.[24] Not all Chinese
migrants were confined at Angel Island, and not everyone confined there was Chinese. In 1913, for example, 76 percent of Angel
Island detainees were Chinese. Most of the rest were Japanese. A
mere 7 percent were not Asian.[25] Race was clearly an important
factor in identifying detention targets. But so too were gender
and class. Chinese women were more likely than men to end up
at Angel Island, presumably because they were more likely to be
pegged as prostitutes. Among passengers of all races, people traveling in steerage were more likely to be detained than were first-class
or second-class passengers.[26]

Among the people detained on Angel Island, Quok Shee stands
out. When she arrived in San Francisco from Hong Kong at the
age of twenty, immigration officials suspected that the man accompanying her, fifty-six-year-old Chew Hoy Quong, was bringing her for immoral purposes. Inspector J.B. Warner grilled each
separately, fishing for discrepancies that might support his suspicion. "How was the bedroom lighted" in the building in which
the couple had allegedly married, the inspector asked. "How was

the parlor furnished? What kind of clock did you have in your parlor?" She recalled its being made of wood. He said it was metal. There were enough discrepancies for immigration officials to deny her admission into the United States. With the help of various San Francisco lawyers, the couple fought back in the courts. But while they did, Quok Shee spent her days at Angel Island. Fifteen months later, her lawyer warned immigration officials that she might kill herself. Still she was denied release. Fortunately, the worst didn't happen. Instead, for almost two years, Quok Shee was held at Angel Island, "imprisoned and detained," as the court order granting her release in August 1918 described it.[27]

Angel Island would serve as an immigration prison for more than two decades after Quok Shee left. After a fire destroyed the facility in August 1940, immigration officials moved the prisoners to the mainland, and Angel Island never again saw use as an immigration prison.[28]

While detention emerged on both coasts, Ellis Island and Angel Island marked different patterns. At the turn of the century, migrants from Europe were arriving in enormous numbers. On Ellis Island, where the bulk of arriving migrants came from Europe, 10 percent of disembarking migrants were detained in 1907, the busiest year in that outpost's history.[29] In those days, to be European wasn't necessarily to be white, and plenty arrived from disfavored classes—Jews as well as newcomers from southern and eastern Europe, for instance—and the Supreme Court's earlier willingness to free civil imprisonment from the restraints of judicial trials meant that immigration detention could quickly be deployed against dissident migrants.

Within sight of Manhattan, Ellis Island is remembered as a gateway for generations of migrants. It has been romanticized as the site where the United States embraced its twentieth-century migrants. "Give me your tired, your poor / Your huddled masses

yearning to breathe free," pleads the Emma Lazarus poem etched
onto the nearby Statue of Liberty. But as is so often the case, the
reality of Ellis Island is much more complicated. The immigration station there certainly welcomed millions of people to their
new home. It also confined many others, especially as more immigrants entered the country from the less-favored southern and
eastern Europe—"morally delinquent" people of "deteriorating
character," one doctor on Ellis Island complained.[30] Through
two substantial immigration-law amendments enacted in the
1920s, Congress tied future migration to past migration. The Immigration Act of 1921 limited migration from any one country
to 3 percent of the number of migrants from that country living
in the United States in 1910. The 1924 law capped per-country
migration to 2 percent of the 1890 figures, giving Great Britain
43 percent of the total, slashing the allotment for southern and
eastern Europeans, and just about excluding Asians.[31] Governed
by a strict quota linked to a period when migration from northern
and western Europe was more common, unauthorized migration
grew.[32] But because legislators' eyes were on disfavored Europeans,
neither law limited migration from Mexico or any other Western
Hemisphere country.

By the early twentieth century, foreign-born radical leftists
also joined the Chinese as favorite targets. In the midst of World
War I, following the success of the Russian Bolshevik Revolution
in 1917, Congress enacted statutes excluding or deporting anar-
chists, communists, and socialists. Almost immediately, leftists
were rounded up, imprisoned, and frequently deported. Planned
to coincide with the Bolshevik Revolution's second anniversary,
a series of raids nationwide orchestrated by Attorney General A.
Mitchell Palmer led to thousands of arrests. It remains unclear exactly how many people were apprehended, "but best estimates are
that some 6,000 warrants of arrest were issued for alien 'reds,' and
4,000 arrests were made." The assistant secretary of labor at the

time, Louis Post, reported that in Boston prisoners were shackled and marched through city streets. Among those caught up in this ordeal was perhaps the most famous leftist of the era, the anarchist Emma Goldman. Automatically stripped of her U.S. citizenship when her husband lost his, she described the migrants forced onto the U.S.S. *Buford*, nicknamed the "Red Ark," as "prisoners."[33] Recalling with horror the realization that she was being shipped out, Goldman described seeing New York from the window of a cramped transport ship: "Through the port-hole I could see the great city receding into the distance, its sky-line of buildings traceable by their rearing heads. It was my beloved city, the metropolis of the New World. It was America, indeed, America repeating the terrible scenes of tsarist Russia! I glanced up—the Statue of Liberty!"[34]

After the federal government started detaining migrants, it wasn't long before courts were asked to weigh in on immigration imprisonment's legality. For a time, the Chinese community of California proved especially adept at tapping the power of the federal courts to limit detention. So many Chinese petitioned the federal trial court in San Francisco for entry into the United States that local newspapers in the 1880s referred to it as a "habeas corpus mill," named after the legal procedure inherited from the British used to challenge the legality of detention.[35] Most, it seems, were successful. Of the approximately four thousand petitions filed between the moment when the Chinese Exclusion Act of 1882 was implemented and January 1888, one newspaper reported, 87 percent were granted permission to enter the United States.[36] For a time, the courts clearly represented a check on the government's newfound detention interest.

Success was short-lived. As was inevitable, the legal fight moved from the trial courts to the Supreme Court. In 1896, the justices emphatically declared that immigration imprisonment was constitutionally permissible. "We think it clear that detention or temporary confinement, as part of the means necessary to give effect to the provisions for the exclusion or expulsion of aliens, would be valid," a unanimous Court announced in *Wong Wing v. United States*.[37] In that short phrase, the Court established civil immigration imprisonment: people can be deprived of their liberty while the government decides if they are to be allowed to remain in the United States. Only a few sentences later, the Court acknowledged criminal immigration imprisonment. "So, too," the Court explained, "we think it would be plainly competent for congress to declare the act of an alien in remaining unlawfully within the United States to be an offense punishable by fine or imprisonment, if such offense were to be established by a judicial trial." For immigration to be punished criminally through confinement, the government must rely on a standard criminal prosecution, including all the protections afforded defendants.

But being subjected to civil authority has never meant escaping prison's cluthes. Among the most famous of those detained at Ellis Island was Ellen Knauff. Born in Germany, she spent part of Hitler's reign in Czechoslovakia. When war caught up with her, she headed to England as a refugee, where she worked for the Royal Air Force, then the United States Army. While helping the Allied forces, she met U.S. citizen and Army veteran Kurt Knauff. After the war, the two married with the approval of the Army's commanding officer in Frankfurt.[38] Taking advantage of the War Brides Act, a special immigration procedure created by Congress precisely to let war veterans return to the United States with their new wives, Ellen arrived in New York on August 14, 1948.

That's when the honeymoon turned to a nightmare. Citing evidence that they refused to disclose even to the Knauffs, immigration officials at Ellis Island were anything but welcoming. Ellen was excluded from the United States and sent to the restrictive quarters of the island's immigration station to fight for her freedom. "As we approached Ellis Island," she later wrote, "I could see that parts of it were enclosed by double wire fences topped by barbed wire and marked by what appeared to be watchtowers. These fenced-off areas were subdivided by more fences which gave the whole place the look of a group of kennels."[39] An official history published by the now-defunct INS described it as "a grueling detention-like penitentiary."[40]

Ellen wasn't even given a hearing at which she might claim her right to enter the United States or plead for mercy.[41] Time and again immigration officials denied Ellen's attempts to live freely in the United States with her husband. Time and again, they cited secret evidence that "her admission would be prejudicial to the interests of the United States." Insistent, she fought all the way to the Supreme Court, where she found little comfort.

The Constitution's promise of a fair hearing proved meaningless. Despite Justice Robert Jackson letting her off Ellis Island in May 1949, his colleagues weren't so sympathetic. For people like Ellen hoping to enter the United States, the Court ruled, Congress can create any procedure it likes. "Whatever the procedure authorized by Congress is, it is due process as far as an alien denied entry is concerned," the Court wrote in January 1950.[42] The next month Ellen was back on the island. Eight decades later, courts continue relying on this line to deny all but the most limited procedural protections to migrants who have not been inspected and legally authorized to enter the United States.[43]

Undeterred, the Knauffs mounted a public-relations campaign, harnessing the power of public sympathy toward veterans and their "war brides." Full-page advertisements supporting Ellen appeared in major newspapers. Editorial writers called for the courts to revisit their position. Members of Congress introduced legislation to help her.[44] After Kurt personally appealed to the attorney general, Ellen was once more let off Ellis Island in January 1951 and, despite not being required to, the attorney general granted her a hearing. Again, she was denied admission as a national security threat and returned to the island prison four months after her release. Government witnesses claimed she was a Communist spy who had given classified information to Czechoslovakian officials. On appeal, she finally obtained the relief she wanted. The government's immigration appeals unit, the Board of Immigration Appeals, concluded that the spying accusations that had resulted in her long imprisonment on Ellis Island were flimsy. They were nothing more than "hearsay, uncorroborated by direct evidence," the appeals board wrote in its official decision.[45] More than three years after Ellen was first held at Ellis Island, the Knauffs were finally able to enter the United States together.

Just three years later, the Supreme Court rejected a lawsuit brought by another Ellis Island prisoner, Ignatz Mezei. Born on the British territory of Gibraltar to parents of "Hungarian or Rumanian" origin, Mezei had lived in the United States for a quarter century when he left in an attempt to see his dying mother in Romania.[46] He never made it. Romania didn't let him in. Instead, he spent roughly nineteen months in Hungary waiting for a visa allowing him to leave. When he finally returned to the United States, he was unceremoniously sent to Ellis Island. As with Ellen Knauff, the world superpower thought him too dangerous to admit. Indeed, too dangerous to know why he was barred and too dangerous to receive a hearing. His time inside the Soviet bloc was enough to minimize his twenty-five years of unremarkable residence in the United States. Fighting all the way to the Supreme Court, he too fared poorly. To the majority of the justices, Ellis Island wasn't a prison. It was "harborage . . . temporary refuge," wrote Justice Tom Clark.[47]

Four of the justice's colleagues disagreed. Justices Hugo Black and William Douglas complained that the government refused to let Mezei visit his wife in Buffalo even temporarily. But it was Justice Robert Jackson, who just years before had led the victorious Allies in prosecuting the most senior Nazi officials at the post-war Nuremberg tribunal, who was most forceful.

His commitment to procedural fairness remained a guide post. Evoking the ancient legal principle that no one should be imprisoned without knowing why, he took issue with the majority of his colleagues, who viewed Ellis Island as a humanitarian refuge. "It overworks legal fiction to say that one is free in law when by the commonest of common sense he is bound," Jackson wrote.[48] Mezei was imprisoned on Ellis Island due to the power of federal immigration officials. To treat the speck of land as a place of safety made no sense to Jackson. "That might mean freedom, if only he were an amphibian!" he wrote in one of the most memorable lines of any Supreme Court decision.[49] Recognizing that he was on the losing end of this argument, he complained that the majority opinion would seem to allow government officials to exclude Mezei by "eject[ing] him bodily into the sea."[50] As far as we know, the government has yet to test Jackson's fear of brutish violence.

Despite embracing immigration imprisonment, the Supreme Court never got around to elaborating its position. Given that all immigration imprisonment targets violations of immigration law, why is the civil type of imprisonment permissible without a judicial trial but its criminal variety is not? Neither the Supreme Court nor the lower courts have ever shed light on this distinction. More than fifty years after *Wong Wing*, the Supreme Court could do no more than repeat itself: "Detention is necessarily a part of this deportation procedure."[51] Viewed with the benefit of hindsight, the Supreme Court's simple conclusion about the procedures required—or not—of immigration imprisonment's two iterations isn't intuitive. The two types of imprisonment are almost identical. From the psychological toll of confinement and invasive security checks to the literal architecture of the facilities used, it is difficult for anyone to see meaningful differences. That was true in the late nineteenth century when dockside sheds were cast as worse than jails. And it is true today.

Just as World War II battles reshaped European landscapes, wartime politics turned foes into friends. Long the focus of harsh discrimination in the United States, Chinese citizens played an instrumental role combatting the Allies' powerful foe in Asia, Japan. Some 14 million Chinese citizens lost their lives during the war.[52] Meanwhile, the United States' broad legal regime of racial discrimination came under attack by African Americans and Latinos, who could die alongside white soldiers on European battlefields but could not dine or study with them in stateside restaurants and universities. In the war's aftermath, these critics did not let up. On the contrary, the pressure intensified when the Soviet Union began using racial discrimination as a rallying point in its search for allies for the emerging Cold War. Numerous countries in Africa, Asia, and Latin America were all too willing to capitalize on the global power struggle to improve their citizens' access to the United States.[53]

Eventually, the United States could no longer ignore its blatantly discriminatory immigration laws. During the mid-1900s, several presidents tried and failed to remove patently racist provisions from immigration law. In 1952, President Harry S. Truman vetoed a proposal that favored migration from northern and western Europe and limited migration from all of Asia to a measly two thousand people per year. Congress overrode his veto.[54] The following year, Truman's Commission on Immigration and Naturalization recommended abolishing racial and national-origin discrimination in immigration law. His successor, Dwight Eisenhower, agreed. As a candidate for president, Eisenhower declared, "We must strike from our statute books any legislation concerning immigration that implies the blasphemy against democracy that only certain Europeans are welcome on American shores." A few months later during his first State of the Union address, he told Congress, "Existing legislation contains injustices. It does, in fact discriminate. . . ."[55] Despite his complaints and stature as a wartime hero, even President Eisenhower was unable to successfully prod Congress to eliminate immigration law's racist sorting mechanism. Where presidents failed, "the critical impetus for dismantling the national-origins quota system in 1965" was the threat of Soviet influence.[56] That year, Congress finally brought national-origins discrimination to an end.

2

ON THE PRISON'S EDGE

Understanding immigration prisons today requires understanding migration. Who comes to the United States, why, and how? People don't flip a coin to decide whether they will leave their home, uproot their family, and start life from scratch. Nor do they pick their destination in a high-stakes game of darts. Migratory paths turn on historical ties. They are triggered by peculiar relationships between individuals and nations. My mother left rural central Mexico for urban northern Mexico because a government program to industrialize border cities had already lured her uncle there. Years later, my mom moved to Texas because my father was already there. And he was there because that's where the jobs were for his father.

Sometimes U.S. foreign policy pushes people to despair, like when the United States supported rightwing governments and paramilitary forces in Central America that destabilized teetering democracies. Sometimes officials just shut their eyes to death and destruction, like with the bodies that dot the Arizona desert. When it comes to the United States and its relationships with Mexico and Central America, where most of today's immigration prisoners were born, the connections run deep. These are different countries, but they share a common history that revolves around migration. With migration comes the possibility of exploitation. Poor people of color are dispossessed of wealth and pushed to the margins of society. Once marginalized, they can be exploited more easily.

For two centuries, law and policing have helped to impoverish Mexicans and exploit their bodies as sources of cheap labor. In the nineteenth and early twentieth centuries, Mexicans living in what is now the western and southwestern United States were routinely murdered by white people. At other times, they were stripped of their land through drawn-out, expensive legal cases or outright terror. Texas's state police force, the Texas Rangers, killed so many Mexicans that one newspaper reported that the "finding of dead bodies of Mexicans . . . creates little or no interest." Witnesses sometimes claimed that Rangers burned their victims alive. "They came in every morning," reported a white South Texas resident, with "the ones that were part dead, they just built up a big fire and burned them up in a brush pile behind this lumber company." [1] Meanwhile, white vigilantes and sheriffs lynched at least six hundred Mexicans, a rate that roughly approximates the number of African Americans lynched during the same period when we account for the different population sizes. [2]

White violence left Mexicans in the West and Southwest vulnerable to economic exploitation. Obviously, the dead could no longer compete for precious natural resources—land, water, and livestock—essential to the region's economic development. Survivors were also affected. But, traumatized by news of murdered friends and relatives, the Mexicans who survived felt the shudder of death any time they might be accused of riling white sensibilities. [3] Pushed off their land and threatened with the most brutal of violence, Mexicans were relegated to a status of an "inferior racial other"—a source of cheap labor heaped at the bottom of the region's racial hierarchy. [4]

Beyond violence, government officials and private employers from the United States encouraged generations of Mexicans and Central Americans to move north. No example is more important than the two-decades-long guest-worker initiative between Mexico and the United States called the Bracero Program. Started in the midst of labor shortages caused by World War II, the Bracero Program led to hundreds of thousands of Mexicans coming to the United States every year with the federal government's blessing. Literally referring to people who work with their arms, the initiative was supported by the political and economic elite of both countries. To the United States, it meant a metaphorical army of low-wage laborers could do the work left behind by the actual army of young men who had been shipped to the battlefields of Europe and Asia. To Mexico, it provided an escape valve. Its young men could work in the United States instead of remaining at home in poverty, where they might be tempted to repeat the revolutionary insurrections of only two decades earlier. Recruiters fanned throughout Mexico to convince young men to head north. Intrepid youth willing to do so would be given transportation, a job, and permission to cross the border.

Without question, the Bracero Program was formally designed to give employers the upper hand. Everyone knew it. Workers were granted permission to come to the United States to work for a specific employer during a particular period, usually a certain harvest season. As a result, they were always subject to the employer's control. Losing a job meant losing legal permission to be in the United States. The threat of being picked up by immigration agents and put on the next bus to Mexico loomed constantly. Braceros, as these temporary laborers were known, were supposed to be paid the usual wage in the region—officially called the prevailing wage—and receive social security contributions. Both requirements were intended to keep bracero labor at roughly the same cost as local labor. The law reflected a desire to let employers get the workers they needed, but not by undercutting homegrown labor.

Both requirements were empty promises. Instead of respecting the legal requirement to treat migrant and native-born workers fairly, the immigration historian Mae Ngai explains, "the Department of Labor determined the 'prevailing wage' by calling local meetings of growers, grower associations, and farm organizations. It made no independent investigation of the labor market and took no input from domestic workers, labor unions, or independent organizations. The prevailing wage was thus whatever growers decided it to be."[5] Getting ripped off by employers violating the spirit and maybe the letter of the law wasn't all. United States government officials and employers also treated braceros horribly. At times, workers were literally fumigated at arm's length. Shirtless, they were herded like cattle into rickety screening sites, where their bodies were sprayed from top to bottom, sometimes with DDT. In Texas, conditions were frequently so bad that, for a time, the Mexican government refused to let employers statewide hire braceros.[6]

I remember asking my grandfather about his bracero experiences when I was a teenager. For a child accustomed to seeing the tall man expertly wield a machete and navigate cornfields with aplomb, his answer remains jarring even two decades later. With a cold gleam in his eyes, he described to me the incessant verbal abuse. He talked about the long hours in the hot sun of my native South Texas, where requests for water were denied with derision. "We had to pee in the fields," he said in Spanish, conveying in his expression the humiliation public urination carried for him, a private, reserved man. I imagined this embodiment of dignity lowering his eyes for want of a simple latrine.

Of all of his descriptions, clearest of all were the words that captured what his experience as a bracero left him feeling about the United States. "Jamas volveré," he said, putting words to the frustrating reality my mother encountered every time she asked him to visit our family in Texas. He vowed never to return to the United States. I recall him going back on those words—a promise he seemed to have made to himself to bear the pain of remembering—twice only: for my oldest sister's quinceñera, the traditional coming-of-age party for Mexican girls, and her wedding. As soon as the festivities were over, while most of us were exhausted and still recovering, my grandfather was on a bus back to Mexico.

Government officials didn't just enact the Bracero Program. They turned the wheels that crushed the dignity of men like my grandfather. The Border Patrol, then and now the nation's main border police force, was intimately involved in helping employers exploit workers. Owners of large farms in Texas, California, and throughout the Southwest often worked directly with Border Patrol agents to ensure that they had the right number—and right kind—of workers at just the right moment. When employers complained of mouthy Mexicans who dared to demand better treatment or higher wages, Border Patrol agents made an appearance. They detained and deported their way to a scared workforce. When employers needed help refreshing the legality of their labor pool, Border Patrol agents escorted migrants to the border. Migrants would be told to cross the border into Mexico, then come right back to the waiting government trucks: a few steps south of the boundary line was enough to start their legal presence in the United States all over. In this way, law enforcement officers took "wetback" laborers to be "dried out."

The Bracero Program was a boon for industries like farming that were dependent on cheap labor, but for Mexican migrant workers it was the bare-faced commodification of their lives. A high-level commission appointed by President Harry S. Truman described the Mexican braceros as "ready to go to work when needed; to be gone when not needed."[7] No concern was given to the poor young men who made up the bulk of the bracero workers as people. It was as if braceros weren't humans who build relationships with other people and who create attachments to places. But friendships do develop, romances bud, families are created, and communities are established. Patterns emerge. Instead of focusing on developing economic activity in their Mexican cities and towns, braceros turned their economic hopes to wage labor in the United States. Their physical energy and ingenuity naturally centered on the possibilities available in places like Texas and California, not San Luis Potosí and Durango.

For many, living in the United States was meant to be temporary. Like my grandfather, some kept to that. Many others found permanent jobs, bought houses, married, and had children. They stopped migrating and became residents of the United States. The younger siblings, distant relatives, and fellow townsfolk of those who came before soon tapped their knowledge to come here themselves, ensuring that the migrant experience remained fresh. My mother's experience illustrates this phenomenon. After meeting my father south of the border, eventually they relocated their young family across the river to what was then the sleepy border town of McAllen, where a few years later I was born.

Unlike my mother, not all migrants who became residents of the United States did so because that was their preference. Traditionally, people came and went as the demands of work and life twisted and tugged—what social scientists call circular migration. It's estimated that as many as six out of ten Italians who came to the United States at the start of the twentieth century returned to Italy.[8] By no means was this unusual. When I was visiting the underground cellars of a small city in Poland, my guide told me his grandfather had lived in the United States before returning to this out-of-the-way town, where a single row of restaurants and bars rings the picture-perfect central plaza. For Mexicans, circular migration was a way of life. Jobs were north of the border, but home was south. But, touted as a temporary vehicle for filling wartime labor shortages, the Bracero Program came to an end in 1964.

In the same way that immigration-law enforcement took a radically different form in the late twentieth century, transformational changes were happening to immigration law too. Instead of outright bans against the Chinese or quotas that favored western and northern Europe, the Immigration Act of 1965 seemed to usher in a new era. The Hart-Celler Act, as the 1965 legislation is commonly called, brought a semblance of equality to federal immigration law. People from every country in Africa, Asia, and Europe were treated the same: each nation could send up to 20,000 people to the United States every year until a cumulative total of 170,000 people had arrived from anywhere in the hemisphere. After that, immigration from the world's Eastern Hemisphere was cut off. Within a few years, long-disfavored Asian countries dominated the United States immigration rolls. Excluding Western Hemisphere countries, four of the top six migrant-originating countries in 1971 were in Asia.[9] This literally changed the look of immigration. Instead of the white faces that had dominated migration from the late nineteenth century onward, late twentieth-century migration was decidedly not white.

Ironically, relaxing limits on migration generally made it harder for Mexicans and Central Americans to come to the United States lawfully. Instead of the relatively unimpeded and welcomed access to the United States that Mexicans and Central Americans had become used to, the Hart-Celler Act applied equal, but less favorable, treatment to the Americas. Every country in the Western Hemisphere could send an unlimited number of people so long as the hemispheric total did not surpass 120,000. On its face, this seemed fair, but on the ground, it was anything but equal. In the early 1960s, there were 200,000 Mexican braceros heading to the United States every year with the federal government's blessing— legal status in one hand, work permit in another. When immigration law changed in 1965, fewer people could come from the entire Western Hemisphere than had been coming from Mexico alone.

The labor market didn't radically transform. Jobs didn't evaporate in the United States and magically pop up in Mexico. Families and friends here didn't suddenly disappear. Mexicans kept coming to the United States, they continued doing the same kind of low-paid work as before, and they kept their ties in the United States and back in Mexico. The only thing that changed was the law. Before, they could do all this legally; suddenly, they couldn't. Immigration law created unauthorized migration from Mexico. In 1976, Congress increased unauthorized migration when it capped Mexican migration at 20,000 people per year. To poor Mexicans who had long been wooed by U.S. businesses and consumers, the Hart-Celler Act's migration ceilings felt like a cruel joke.

The civil rights era's emphasis on formal equality replaced blatantly discriminatory laws and pushed the nation closer to its democratic aspirations. But perversely, the Hart-Celler Act's formal equality turned immigration law against Mexican migrants. Instead of opening paths into the United States, the 1965 law's emphasis on treating everyone equally meant that there was no appreciation for the unique events leading many Mexicans to the United States. These liberalizing amendments simply turned Mexicans into the picture of immigration lawlessness. Mexican migrants, writes the immigration historian Mae Ngai, were "recast . . . as 'illegal.'"[10] In this way, most Mexican and Central American migrants today stand on different ground than those from generations past. Instead of choosing to flout established pathways into the United States, most Mexican and Central American migrants use the only pathways realistically available, legal or not.

Meanwhile, under Eisenhower's watch, the INS had all but abandoned its detention policy in 1954. This was not a fluke but rather the result of deliberate policy choices. Announcing the policy shift, the attorney general said this was a step toward a "humane administration of the immigration laws."[11] Writing for a majority of the Supreme Court, Justice Tom Clark, a man who had coordinated the forced internment of Japanese Americans during World War II, commented that the government's no-detention policy "reflects the humane qualities of an enlightened civilization." And for the next quarter century, few migrants were confined at any point. When confinement did occur, it was short-lived; most people were released while immigration courts heard their cases.[12] In fact if not in law, the United States came remarkably close to abolishing immigration imprisonment.

When I talk about the Eisenhower government's ending detention, modern audiences eye me suspiciously. And yet it happened. When the time came for the Ellis Island detention facility to shut down, Attorney General Herbert Brownell said matter-of-factly that "the little island between the Statue of Liberty and the skyline and piers of New York seems to have served its purpose." That day, the *New York Times* reported, "the last detained alien—a Norwegian seaman who had overstayed his shore leave—was a passenger on the Battery-bound ferry. . . ."[13] Even though this Norwegian seaman had evidently violated immigration law, he entered Manhattan with the federal government's permission, promising to leave the United States soon. In all likelihood, we will never know whether he did. Enforcement efforts were sporadic, and record-keeping dismal. There is a good chance he disappeared into the masses of humanity teeming in mid-century New York. Perhaps he stayed there. Perhaps he made a life in some other corner of the newly invigorated post-war nation. Some reports suggest he might have become a U.S. citizen. Whatever might have happened, he marks an important juncture in the history of immigration imprisonment. When the doors of the Ellis Island detention center clanged shut after his departure, they never reopened for another soul, and the doors of immigration prisons would not begin to open and close routinely for a quarter century.

The United States of the mid-1950s was certainly different from today's version in many respects, but there was not a radically different vision of migrants. Scapegoating and demonizing were rampant then as they are now. Indeed, the very same year that the INS shuttered most of its detention operations, the prestigious academic journal the *Stanford Law Review* published an article titled "Wetbacks: Can the States Act to Curb Illegal Entry?"[14] There was no effort to shy away from the demeaning, racist term "wetback." That year and the next, the INS, with the cooperation of Mexican authorities, launched "Operation Wetback."[15] Under the new leadership of retired general Joseph Swing, a "longtime Mexican hater," the INS's enforcement strategy was patterned after military campaigns. It featured quick mobilization of large forces to stop migrants from entering the United States and rounding up those already inside.[16] Throwing into overdrive tactics the INS had been using over the previous decade, agents arrested Mexicans throughout the Southwest and in cities like Chicago that had large Mexican populations, forced them onto trucks and trains, and deported them. Driven by a single-minded desire to maintain Mexicans as disposable laborers, INS officials handed deportees to waiting Mexican officials, who promptly sent them into the Mexican interior "where work was plentiful."[17] Neither INS officials nor their Mexican counterparts seemed to care much about who they actually targeted. Among the deported were an unknown number of U.S. citizens.[18]

Why did the United States shift away from detention despite widespread animus of Mexicans and a history of confinement? The answer lies in convenience and self-interest rather than altruism. Immigration prisons are expensive to the federal government, which pays the cost of buildings, guards, and food. By 1954, when the INS announced that it would end detention except in extraordinary situations, Angel Island had burned down and Ellis Island was in need of repair. Closing the Ellis Island prison saved the government $900,000, Attorney General Herbert Brownell reportedly claimed, about $8.5 million in 2018 dollars.[19]

Immigration prisons are also enormously costly to the businesses that would otherwise be tapping migrants as cheap labor. Just like today, major industries in the mid-twentieth century relied on poor workers to bring products to market and keep office doors open. After the stock-market collapse of 1929, low-wage workers and poor farmers headed west, forever memorialized by Dorothea Lange's 1936 photograph *Migrant Mother* and John Steinbeck's *Grapes of Wrath*, published in 1939. Within a few years, most of the world was facing off in battles across Europe and Asia. In the United States, young men joined the military, leaving space for white women to join the paid workforce in large numbers. Like Naomi Parker Fraley, the real-life inspiration for the World War II–era "Rosie the Riveter" posters, they tended toward the urban industrial activity powering the war effort.

In the rural fields where the nation's food supply grew, the picture was markedly different. There, migrants, mostly from Mexico, arrived to pick cotton, pluck apples, and tend grapevines. The five million Mexicans who came to the United States between 1942 and 1964 under the auspices of the Bracero Program almost all headed to the fields. During the 1950s, while war raged in Korea, braceros made up over half of the workers picking labor-intensive crops like oranges and tomatoes in California.[20]

Keeping workers in the fields was essential to the business of agriculture. Prisons were not compatible with an agricultural industry newly dependent on cheap migrant labor. After all, a migrant who was locked up was a migrant who could not work. To keep employers happy, officials typically kept themselves in the dark about immigration-law violations. Policing of the border was sparse. The Border Patrol didn't exist until 1924, and around the middle of the century, the agency could count on no more than 1,800 agents to patrol the nation's boundaries.[21] Imprisoning migrants would defeat the purpose of employers' and government officials' efforts.

Back then the law helped make migrants "ready to go to work when needed; to be gone when not needed," and it does so now as well. Immigration officials are authorized to question anyone they think is not a U.S. citizen about their immigration status. If they are unconvinced that a person has the government's permission to be in the United States, they can arrest and start the deportation process. Ordinarily, the federal government's power to stop and question people is curtailed by the Fourth Amendment. The politically and economically powerful men who led the young nation in the late eighteenth century were well aware of the frightening prospects of unimpeded law enforcement. Added to the federal Constitution in response to the British monarch's practice of barging into people's homes and workplaces searching for evidence of wrongdoing, the Fourth Amendment served as a simple obstacle between the people and the government. If law enforcement officers want to prevent someone from going about their day, they need to have actual evidence of wrongdoing.

To breathe life into the suspicion requirement, they mandated how much suspicion. A hunch is not enough. This is the Fourth Amendment's famous probable-cause requirement. "The right of the people to be secure in their persons, houses, papers, and effects, against unreasonable searches and seizures, shall not be violated, and no warrants shall issue, but upon probable cause," the amendment's simple language reads. Law enforcement officers can get a warrant only if they convince a judge that they have gathered evidence that the person targeted committed a crime. It is a powerful limitation on the government's power.

When I cover the Fourth Amendment in my law school classes, I push my students to consider their reaction to police arriving at their workplace. Imagine yourself in this situation, I tell them: You are at work one day. Your workplace, like many others, consists of rows of individual workstations. There are about forty people who work with you. Without warning, police officers suddenly rush through the three entrances into the building. Immediately, some officers position themselves by all the exits—the doors, emergency exits, and windows. You guess there are between fifteen and twenty-five cops. They are shouting "police" and wearing police uniforms and badges. The officers who are not positioned at the exits start to move through the building, going workstation to workstation from the front of the office to the back, asking questions of everyone. Because your workstation is toward the back, you can't hear what they're asking, but you can see that most people are asked a few questions—you guess three or four—before the officers move on. Some people reach into their purses or wallets to take out papers or what look like identification cards, they hand them to the officers, and then the officers move on. Other people, though, are being handcuffed and escorted out the door that leads to the parking lot. Later, I tell my students, you learn that they were being put into police vans. While you're busy trying to look like you're doing your work, you notice that the officers are all carrying guns. Do you feel like you can leave or refuse to speak to the officers?

This scenario is not my invention. Replace the police officers with INS agents, put everyone inside the now-defunct Davis Pleating and Button Company in Los Angeles, take a step back in time to 1977, and these details come from the Supreme Court's recounting of the events that led to its decision in *INS v. Delgado*. In that case, the Court announced that the people who suddenly found their worksite overrun by INS agents had not been deprived of the freedom to move about as they liked. In the language of the Fourth Amendment, they had not been "seized," because a reasonable person in that situation would think they could leave or end the encounter with the officers. The Court explained that if the workers' freedom of movement was restricted, it was restricted by their "voluntary obligations to their employer."[22] It was the need to make money that kept them there; not the swarm of armed INS agents. As for the officers positioned at the doors, even though their "obvious presence . . . was to insure that all persons in the factories were questioned . . . the mere possibility that they would be questioned if they sought to leave the buildings should not have resulted in any reasonable apprehension by any of them that they would be seized or detained in any meaningful way."[23] *Delgado* remains good law.

Delgado wasn't the only case. The year before a mass of INS agents raided Davis Pleating, two of their colleagues visited a car repair shop in San Mateo, California, just south of where San Francisco International Airport now sits. They wanted to look around and talk to some of the mechanics about their immigration status. Despite the Fourth Amendment's expectation that law enforcement agents must obtain a warrant, they didn't have one. For his part, the owner, in the words of former Supreme Court Justice Sandra Day O'Connor, "firmly refused to allow the agents to interview his employees."[24] Nonetheless, the agents won out. While one distracted the owner—what Justice O'Connor politely describes as "engaged the proprietor in conversation"—another walked into the shop and began questioning Adán López-Mendoza. Soon, López-Mendoza was under arrest by the INS agent, and eventually the government tried to deport him based on statements he made to them.[25] Insisting he had been arrested in violation of the Fourth Amendment, he took his deportation fight all the way to the Supreme Court. That constitutional requirement, the Court announced, has little relevance in immigration courts. The immigration courts, Justice O'Connor wrote, "correctly ruled that 'the mere fact of an illegal arrest has no bearing on a subsequent deportation proceeding.'"[26] Pages later,

Justice O'Connor added two exceptions: an illegal arrest might be problematic if it was "egregious" or an example of "widespread" unconstitutional policing.[27] Ordinary or one-off constitutional violations are acceptable when deciding who should be picked out of their workplace and deported.

While the Supreme Court's decisions in *Delgado* and *López-Mendoza* identify how far immigration-law enforcement veers from ordinary constitutional principles, the underlying facts are not especially unusual. Historically, workplace raids are anything but uncommon. Meanwhile, migrant workers have had a hard time finding passionate defenders, even among likely allies in the labor movement. For most of the nineteenth and twentieth centuries, unions stood more closely aligned with employers and government officials than with migrants. Rather than fend off government targeting of vulnerable laborers, many unions actually fanned the flames of xenophobia. They wanted more government interventions to pick off migrant workers, whom they viewed, in the most charitable light, as cheap alternatives to native-born workers. Just as often, unions voiced their concerns in blatantly racist terms. They complained of heathen "coolies" from China and backward "hunkies" from Hungary. Even the famed United Farm Workers Union, led by César Chávez and Dolores Huerta, cleaved migrants into two camps: legal and illegal. The former, it claimed, should be treated humanely; the latter should be rounded up and deported.[28]

Welcomed as low-paid workers, immigrants were constantly reminded of their precarious position in the United States. They lived with the fear that employers might team up with immigration officials. They faced the reality that, in the immigrant workplace, the Fourth Amendment is a distant dream. They were aware that their obvious allies in the labor movement saw them as threats. Arrest, imprisonment, and deportation existed as part of the calculus of fear. For most, it was a threat, not a reality. But fear matters.

3

THE RESURGENCE OF
IMMIGRATION PRISONS

The waning of immigration imprisonment in the middle of the twentieth century didn't happen in a vacuum. In the 1960s and 1970s, the country's experiment with incarceration was rapidly losing favor. In 1975, a little-known social services worker in Kentucky, Calvin Dodge, spearheaded an impressive collection of essays announcing a path toward prison abolition. "Imprisonment as a primary sanction should be eliminated," Dodge wrote simply and emphatically. It sounds delusional today, decades into a national love affair with forced confinement. Prisons in the United States teetered toward extinction, and impossible as it may be to believe, the United States was on the verge of becoming "a nation without prisons."[1]

The contributors whom Dodge assembled were no collection of radical leftists. They were staid professionals well within the mainstream: academics, a judge, and even a presidential commission appointed by none other than Richard Nixon. A research group with links to the Justice Department claimed "there [is] reason . . . for hope that America might lead the world away from the use of cages for criminals."[2] Its abolitionist tone was unmistakable. Humans could not rightfully be caged. Lodging a brutal critique of prisons, the Nixon-created National Advisory Commission on Criminal Justice Standards wrote, "[The prison] is obsolete, cannot be reformed, should not be perpetuated through the false hope of forced 'treatment'; it should be repudiated as useless for

any purpose other than locking away persons who are too dangerous to be allowed at large in free society."[3] In this moment in the
nation's history, prisons were the past, not the future. "By the mid-
1970s," writes the sociologist Loïc Wacquant, "a broad consensus
had formed . . . according to which the future of the prison in the
United States was anything but bright."[4]

The United States of the early 1970s held roughly a quarter-
million people in all prisons and jails. Today, there are almost that
many serving life sentences, with more than 2.2 million people
locked up. Far outpacing the willingness of other countries to
imprison its residents, clearly the Commission's declaration of
the prison's uselessness lost favor. It wouldn't be until 2003 when
someone else prominently took up the abolitionist cause. When
that happened, it came from Angela Davis, the radical leftist intellectual and former political prisoner who once found herself on
the FBI's list of Ten Most Wanted Fugitives.[5]

The nation's transformation from a country on the verge of
dismantling prisons to one that puts them at the center of social
planning was not limited to the common focus of advocates and
policymakers: people caught up in the war on drugs. On the contrary, the nation's well-known fetishization of imprisonment is the
result of a wholesale restructuring of social relations. It has swept
up the African American men targeted by anti-drug policies, to be
sure, but it does not end there.

Like the more familiar drug-war policies, the modern era of
immigration imprisonment began in the decades following the
civil rights struggles of the 1960s and 1970s. Successful efforts
to ban blatant displays of discrimination required changes in the
law and, equally significant, in culture. The Civil Rights Act of
1964 and the Voting Rights Act of 1965 marked major legal vic-
tories and ushered in a new era, one in which the old racial hierarchy was both illegal and morally indefensible. To a limited degree,
that hopeful vision came to pass. People of color could tap legal

remedies defensively—for example, to fight discrimination in public accommodations—and offensively—for example, to enroll in college.

But old ways die hard, and the post–civil rights decades illustrated that the ideology of white supremacy that was entrenched in law and culture did not suddenly disappear and did not exempt immigration.

The civil rights reforms of the mid-twentieth century were accompanied by a tumult in social relations. The Black Panther Party, Southern Christian Leadership Conference, Brown Berets, and American Indian Movement catapulted confrontational civil rights activism onto televisions and newspaper front pages. Schools became sites of protest, and churches became cradles of dissent. Few could miss the upheaval in social relations happening day by day. Coming at the same time as sustained anti-war protests were pushing the United States out of its bloody conflict in Vietnam and political giants like Martin Luther King Jr. and the Kennedy brothers were being assassinated, it seemed as if the United States was being unglued. The old ways of being were challenged, decried as morally debased, and upended.

In the rhetorical struggle between civil rights and law and order, racism was pushed just beneath the surface of law and culture. In a stunningly short period of time, crime took race's position as the recognized socially acceptable marker of dangerousness, and concern about crime rates became the public face of racism. Before becoming famous for his opposition to integration, Alabama's Governor George Wallace made a name for himself by linking civil rights activism to a perceived breakdown in law and order. Other politicians and political strategists soon picked up on the tactic as a way of currying favor with disaffected white Americans.

But no one was nearly as successful as Richard Nixon. Trying to win the White House, Nixon hoped to capitalize on white disaffection with the quakes rattling U.S. law and culture. "The Nixon campaign in 1968, and the Nixon White House after that, had two enemies: the antiwar left and black people," the disgraced Nixon official John Ehrlichman told a reporter years later. "We knew we couldn't make it illegal to be either against the war or black, but by getting the public to associate the hippies with marijuana and blacks with heroin, and then criminalizing both heavily, we could disrupt those communities. We could arrest their leaders, raid their homes, break up their meetings, and vilify them night after night on the evening news. Did we know we were lying about the drugs? Of course we did."[6] Ehrlichman's admission sounds too honest to be true. Few people would be so open about their moral depravity. But Ehrlichman had already shown himself to be a man of few scruples. He was, in the words of his *New York Times* obituary, "Nixon's pugnacious defender" who went to prison for his involvement in Watergate.

Tapping fears of crime, as Ehrlichman suggests, was a powerful political ploy. Before the Nixon administration paired social decay with drug use and civil rights activism, few people in the United States had concerned themselves about crime, even as crime rates rose in the 1960s as the baby-boom generation reached the main years during which adults commit crimes. With Nixon at the helm, politicians began to harp about the crime ravaging U.S. cities. Eventually, discussions of crime among the political elite spread to the broader public, resulting in more widespread concern about crime, especially illicit drug activity. By the time President Reagan grabbed the anti-crime banner to launch his well-known "war on drugs," the U.S. public was primed to embrace the drug-fighting hysteria that dominated the last decades of the twentieth century.[7]

The anti-crime sentiment of the 1960s, 1970s, and 1980s had a lasting effect precisely because it arose as a substitute for the racism that could no longer be expressed as openly. Instead of misguided youth, the criminals of the late twentieth century were depicted as "incorrigible" perpetrators with little hope for redemption. These "young minority males, caught up in the underclass world of crime, drugs, broken families, and welfare dependency," as sociologist David Garland summarized the dominant rhetoric of the time, were "desperate, driven, and capable of mindless violence."[8] Twisting fact into fear, politicians depicted them as vicious savages. George H.W. Bush propelled himself into the White House by showcasing Willie Horton, a black man who had fled a weekend-release program in Massachusetts and raped a white woman, in an ad against the state's governor and Democratic presidential candidate, Michael Dukakis. Eight years later, then first lady Hillary Clinton portrayed gang members as psychopaths. "They are not just gangs of kids anymore," she told a New Hampshire audience in 1996, harkening to a bygone era when troubled youth could be expected to reform. "They are often the kinds of kids that are called superpredators—no conscience, no empathy."[9] In the new penology, these superpredators had a target. Despite the fact that blacks are more likely to be crime victims, middle-class white suburbanites became idealized as the victims of the new crime wave.[10]

The war on crime—and its drug-focused leading edge— became a seemingly intractable feature of law and policy. In the 1980s and 1990s, a new generation of policing philosophies emerged to address the political rhetoric's attention to the ostensibly extreme danger of the new criminality. Nothing emblematizes this policing trend better than the "broken windows theory" popularized in a 1982 magazine article by James Q. Wilson and George L. Kelling. Minor incidents, Wilson and Kelling posited, are the start of much greater lawlessness. If left unattended, a single broken window will soon be joined by a building full of broken windows. Worse is likely to follow. Police should engage in "order-maintenance" tactics that view the most trivial of offenses against public order as nothing short of the start down the long

road toward chaos and violence.[11] Everything is a priority, at least
if the offender is poor and not white. They should do what they
must to stop it.

At the same time, prominent legislators attacked the neutral-
ity of the judicial process. Instead of a criminal justice triangle in
which the prosecutor, representing the whole of the community,
faces off against the defendant under the watchful eye of the neu-
tral judge, the gap between defendants and judges was thought
to have closed. "The judge remains a figure of suspicion, a person
with a propensity to violate public safety, little different in public
confidence from the figure of the criminal before them," wrote legal scholar Jonathan Simon.[12] The new criminal threat, then, was
not coming only from moral deviants. The politicians and pundits
claiming to represent the endangered law-abiding citizenry also
came to view judges suspiciously.

In response, legislatures across the country began stripping
judges of discretion to identify a suitable sentence for convicted
offenders. Led by Congress, legislatures adopted fixed sentencing
ranges and mandatory minimum prison terms. In 1984, Congress
ordered the creation of the United States Sentencing Commission
and charged it with developing sentencing guidelines for judges'
use. That year, the state of Washington adopted a sentencing
scheme in which convicted offenders were required to serve a pre-
determined percentage of their prison sentence before becoming
eligible for release. Called "truth-in-sentencing" laws, these man-
dates exploded in popularity after 1994, when Congress dangled
the promise of grants for new prisons to states that required offenders serve at least 85 percent of their sentence.

More people were prosecuted, they faced longer sentences,
more people went to jail, and there were fewer ways out before
the sentence ran its course. By the end of the 1990s, the nation's
prison population had skyrocketed. Over the next fifteen years, it
kept growing.

The same anti-drug hysteria that swept criminal policing took hold in immigration law. Much like inner-city black men, migrants were depicted as depraved purveyors of death and moral decay, especially those from south of the border. In 1980, for example, 125,000 Cubans who set off from the port of Mariel reached Florida on rickety rafts after the Cuban government announced that anyone who wanted to leave could do so. Unlike earlier generations of Cuban migrants, these so-called *marielitos* were largely poor and dark-skinned, and in the dominant discourse of the day, they were depicted as cast-offs from Castro's prisons. *U.S. News & World Report* ran a story in 1984 emblazoned with the headline "Castro's 'Crime Bomb' Inside U.S." Soon Hollywood added to the factually inaccurate hysteria. In the 1980s blockbuster and cult classic *Scarface*, an adaptation of the 1932 film of the same name, Al Pacino plays Tony Montana, a bloodthirsty psychopath willing to kill just about anyone to rise to the top of Miami's drug world. The film's opening scene expressly connects Pacino's character to the Mariel exodus. Castro, the film claims in text that flashes on the screen, used the Mariel incident to send "the dregs of his jails" to the United States.

Cubans may have dominated sensational media depictions of migrant involvement in criminal activity, but they did not monopolize the political rhetoric. Haitians and Jamaicans were said to be bringing drugs into the United States, with Colombians being no better. "Jamaicans," claimed Representative Lamar Smith in 1987, "mostly illegal aliens, have developed a massive criminal organization that imports and distributes narcotics."[13]

Federal officials tapped their law enforcement powers to control the perceived threat that migrants posed. The Mariel Cubans were sent to federal penitentiaries. That infamous *U.S. News & World Report* article from 1984 captured their treatment in a caption accompanying a photograph of two Cubans that explained that they were incarcerated in a Georgia federal prison. To accommodate Cubans and Haitians, who were also fleeing a totalitarian government, the INS opened the Krome Avenue Detention Center in Miami, a facility that remains operational today. "Detention of aliens seeking asylum was necessary to discourage people like the Haitians from setting sail in the first place," said Attorney General William French Smith in 1982. That year, President Reagan ordered the INS to detain all Haitians who arrived in the United States clandestinely.[14] Soon, Haitian migrants were filling military bases, federal prisons, and prison-like INS detention centers.

Expansion wasn't without controversy. A Republican U.S. senator from Texas opposed a proposed immigration prison on blatantly racist grounds: "You have tripled the black population of Big Springs, Texas, and not even advised me in advance," John Tower complained to Reagan administration officials, citing an earlier transfer of Haitians into a federal prison situated in a rural town. For different reasons, the White House's Office of Management and Budget was skeptical. In internal deliberations, it expressed reservations about the INS's ability to manage a large detention facility. It also cautioned that detention might beget detention. Expanding the INS's capacity to detain, OMB warned, "may encourage INS to detain aliens longer in order to justify the facility's need."[15]

Meanwhile, migration from Central America grew. Midway through the century, Central America had become a site for proxy battles between the United States and the Soviet Union. To escape the bloodshed in countries like El Salvador, Nicaragua, and Guatemala in the 1980s, millions of people sought refuge in the United States. They viewed the powerhouse to the north as a beacon of safety and opportunity.

Reagan administration officials, however, depicted them as Marxist-aligned peasants disrespectful of our laws and ideologically dangerous to our way of life. Standing alongside insurgent *contras* waging a U.S.-backed rebellion against the leftist Sandinista government in Nicaragua, in 1986 President Reagan left no doubt about his view of the region's precarious strategic importance. Soviet allies in Nicaragua, he warned, were "just two days' driving time from Harlingen, Texas," about fifteen minutes south of where today's Willacy County immigration prison sits.[16] Arriving at the nation's southern border, migrants were met with the beginnings of today's vast immigration prison system. The INS ramped up its policing resources as it tried to keep migrants confined to the border region that the agency itself referred to as federal "reservations," evoking the treatment of native people during the period of westward expansion. South Texas became so heavily policed for a time that the U.S. senator Lloyd Bentsen went so far as to call it a "massive detention camp." At the same time, federal officials deliberately rejected as many claims as possible. The INS denied an astonishing 97 percent of asylum petitions by Salvadorans and 99 percent filed by Guatemalans until prolonged legal challenges forced them to consider every application on its own merit.[17]

Jenny Flores was one of those. Her birthplace, El Salvador, was in the midst of war when fifteen-year-old Jenny headed north in 1985. There, she hoped to reunite with her aunt, a U.S. citizen. Instead, the INS locked her up in a converted hotel surrounded by concertina wire. As was routine, she was forced to remove her clothing and was searched. Decades later, her legacy lives on. She is the named plaintiff in the case that still sets the bar for the government's treatment of detained children.

Even now, with the Cold War long over, the violence and political instability that the United States was involved in continues to impact life in the region. Many of the children displaced by Central America's violence in the 1980s and 1990s wound up in the United States. In cities decimated by deindustrialization and racism, they assimilated into urban America's budding gang culture.

MS-13, the transnational gang that Presidents Obama and Trump frequently rail against, got its start in this environment. For some young people, gang membership led to crime, followed by deportation. Born in San Salvador, but bred in Los Angeles, Borromeo Henríquez Solórzano was deported to the country of his birth, but not before joining MS-13 in its early days. Now dubbed El Diablito, Little Devil, he's said to be at the top of the MS-13 hierarchy. The U.S. government thinks he's so influential that in 2013 the Treasury froze his assets.[18] On the backs of these refugees-turned-deportees, MS-13 expanded to Central America, only to return to the United States to complete the circle. Everywhere, MS-13 upends lives, forcing young people across Central America these days to choose between recruitment, violence, or migration.

Mexicans were also part of this great migration north. The political and economic elite of both the United States and Mexico partnered to push large swaths of the Mexican population onto the migratory path northward. In the 1980s, the two countries collaborated on the development of a border-region manufacturing industry. Known as *maquiladoras*, these plants recruited Mexican youth from farther south to staff high-demand assembly processes piecing together common items like car parts and TV screens. Once in view of the United States, many internal migrants eventually continued north. Similarly, the North American Free Trade Agreement, launched in 1994 by Canada, Mexico, and the United States, made traditional subsistence farming more difficult for a generation of young Mexicans, leaving them little choice but to head to Mexican cities or, frequently, the United States to hire themselves out as inexpensive wage laborers.[19]

During the last quarter century of the twentieth century, millions made the United States their home. Soon, familiar patterns emerged. Young people, mostly men, would head north, following networks of relatives and friends. They worked the citrus groves of Florida, the onion fields of South Texas, the vegetable farms of California, even the apple orchards of Washington and the neat rows of Idaho's famous potatoes, helping explain how a batch of my cousins was born near Boise. After decades of migration to the United States, ordinary life developed around this pattern. Economic development in the countries that migrants came from relied on earnings from the United States, and migration became a sort of rite of passage in some communities.

Traditional movement back and forth, year after year, had become increasingly difficult starting in the 1980s, when the INS sent more law enforcement agents and money to South Texas, but circular migration plummeted after 1996, when Democratic president Bill Clinton worked with a Republican Congress to radically boost the federal government's border-policing forces. From 1995 to 2000, the number of Border Patrol agents doubled from roughly 4,000 to over 8,000.[20] This left unauthorized migrants with an impossible choice. Continuing their circular migration pattern might mean never coming back. Either the newly bolstered Border Patrol might catch you or, worse, the desert would. In one fifteen-year period, a single government agency, the Pima County Medical Examiner in Tucson, dealt with the bodies of 2,615 migrants who had lost their lives crossing the Arizona desert.[21]

The alternative was to stay put in the United States, as many did. From 1986 to 2006, the number of migrants living in the United States without the federal government's permission quadrupled from a population of roughly 3 million to a population of 12 million. Migrants came clandestinely but didn't leave. All the while, border policing skyrocketed. The federal government allocated more money and employed more Border Patrol agents, who, in turn, spent more time trying to catch people sneaking into the United States. In a detailed study of Mexican migrants, the researchers Doug Massey, Jorge Durand, and Karen Pren found that increasing border enforcement didn't impact the likelihood

that migrants could cross the border. The trip became more difficult and more expensive, but the outcome didn't change. People
got across just as often as they had before the United States began
pouring money into border policing. Only now, they stayed in the
north.[22]

Effectively stuck in the United States, without any way of le-
galizing their immigration status, they became easily exploited,
with repercussions that can be seen to this day. Like with braceros, employers have the upper hand. Migrants are left to work
under the table or under false pretenses, either of which can lead
to ICE's showing up to make an arrest. The low unionization
rate in the United States means that traditional sources of labor
power are largely ineffectual. And thanks to a 2002 Supreme
Court decision, employers aren't even liable for backpay if they
fire unauthorized workers who dare unionize.[23] Rather than reducing unauthorized migration, more border enforcement means
more unauthorized migrants will be cheaper for employers.

In their border-enforcement study, Massey and his colleagues
described a "tax" that unauthorized migrants were forced to pay as
policing increased. Once the path northward became more dangerous, it became necessary to hire professional smugglers. That
raised the cost of the actual trip. Unable to move around as easily,
migrants couldn't compete for higher wages by leaving for a new
job. Instead, to land jobs, they had to rely on middlemen, who expected to get a cut that previously would've gone to the migrants
themselves. As a result, they earned 25 percent less after border
policing increased than they had in the years before.[24] More border policing didn't mean fewer migrants. More border policing
just meant more profit from border policing.

Police officials, politicians, and academics think of broken-
windows policing as a feature of crime fighting. But a variant of

its focus on low-level infractions appeared in immigration law in the 1980s and 1990s, creating the foundation for the modern legal architecture of immigration imprisonment. Beginning in the mid-1980s, Congress regularly made it easier to confine migrants. Through the Anti-Drug Abuse Act of 1986, for example, Congress set the legal groundwork for immigration detainers, requests from immigration authorities to local police asking them to keep a particular person locked up so that federal officials could move forward with an immigration case. Since then, detainers have come to be a central tool for sweeping people from local custody to ICE detention. In 2011 alone, ICE officers sent 310,000 detainer requests to state prisons and local jails. Illustrating detainers' continued relevance, eight years later, three justices of the Supreme Court complained that "state and local officials sometimes rebuff the Government's request that they give notice when a criminal alien will be released."[25]

Detainers are important, but other developments also contributed to the growing incarceration of migrants. Two years after enacting the detainer legislation, the Anti-Drug Abuse Act of 1988 added the concept of the "aggravated felony" into the immigration-law lexicon. Originally defined to include only a small handful of serious offenses (murder, illicit trafficking in firearms, and drug trafficking), the aggravated felony concept now includes twenty-one subparts—some with their own subparts. The label is as sinister as it is misleading. Justice Samuel Alito and four of his conservative colleagues on the Supreme Court claimed that this includes "certain dangerous crimes."[26] Instead of being limited to the worst offenses, the list of aggravated felonies includes misdemeanors and crimes that few would describe as severe; tax fraud and shoplifting make the list. Reflecting the era's skepticism of judges, Congress denied immigration judges the discretion to release anyone convicted of an aggravated felony. Everyone convicted of an aggravated felony in the last three decades has been detained. This was the beginning of modern mandatory detention for immigrants.

Not content to stop there, in 1990 Congress made it easier for the INS to take hold of people convicted of state drug offenses.[27] In 1994, the very law that Hillary Clinton was defending when she made her "superpredators" comment required the construction of two detention centers for "criminal aliens" and created a reimbursement program that incentivizes local law enforcement inquiries about immigration status. In 2017, the reimbursement program, called the State Criminal Alien Assistance Program, handed $190 million to 680 cities and counties.

To round out the decade, in 1996 Congress adopted two laws that, combined, produced a "seismic change" in immigration detention.[28] The Anti-terrorism and Effective Death Penalty Act expanded the mandatory detention requirement to include all controlled substances. Later that year, the Illegal Immigration Reform and Immigrant Responsibility Act (IIRIRA) expanded mandatory detention again. That law facilitated federal immigration officials' collaborations with state and local police through newly created 287(g) agreements. Under these, state and local cops are essentially deputized to act as federal immigration officers. Arizona's lightning rod of a sheriff Joe Arpaio took advantage of this to illegally target Latinos, leading the Obama Justice Department to end its relationship with him. Eventually, Arpaio lost his job. But Arpaio's demise didn't spell the 287(g) program's end. In the spring of 2018, seventy-eight agencies in twenty states had formal agreements with ICE in effect.

Phat Dinh Truong's legal battle illustrates how quickly and dramatically immigration law came to embrace criminal law in the 1980s and 1990s. Born in Vietnam in 1954, the same year in which Ho Chi Minh's communist forces prevailed against the French and the United States threw its support behind Ngo Dinh

Diem's anticommunist government in the south, Truong came to the United States as a twenty-seven-year-old refugee and soon became a lawful permanent resident. A few years later, in 1985, he committed robbery and was eventually convicted. It appears that he stayed out of trouble after that incident, and still immigration officials tried deporting him ten years later when he returned from a business trip to China. When he committed the crime, no one had ever heard of an aggravated felony. It wouldn't become part of immigration law for another three years. But by the time he returned to the United States from China, immigration law had come to include robbery in its growing list of aggravated felonies requiring confinement and deportation. Unlike criminal law, immigration law lets legislators raise the stakes of illegal activity even years later.[29]

Supporting the industry that gave immigration prisons their start, IIRIRA also included a requirement that the INS—now ICE—consider leasing or purchasing existing detention facilities over building its own. To private prison entrepreneur Tom Beasley, remember, selling prisons is like selling hamburgers. IIRIRA is a reminder that it's a lot easier to sell hamburgers if you force hungry people to browse the menu at McDonald's.

Whether tied to a dangerous ideology, unwanted drug activity, or simply a morally depraved unwillingness to comply with legal requirements, the migrants of the 1980s were framed as voluntary wrongdoers. They had chosen to align with Marxist rebels or drug traffickers. They had elected to become common criminals. At best, they were economic migrants who lacked respect for the rule of law. Regardless, none deserved an open-armed embrace. And none received it.

When the Reagan administration first turned to prisons to address migration, it sent a young Justice Department lawyer, future New York City mayor Rudolph Giuliani, to Capitol Hill.

Pitching the administration's plans to Congress, Giuliani said it needed $35 million to build two prisons. "This additional space is urgently needed if we are able to adequately enforce our immigration laws," he claimed in 1982. Congressman Robert Kastenmeier, a Wisconsin Democrat, wasn't easily convinced. "From 1954 until last summer," the congressman said, "the United States followed a general policy of releasing aliens pending immigration matters. . . . This was, and still is, a wise policy."[30] Eventually, of course, Giuliani's position won, and a radical transition in immigration policy began.

The new century did not bring any break from the rhetoric of migrant criminality that had come to dominate political conversations in the 1980s and 1990s. The extraordinary demands of the days immediately following September 11, 2001, led to extraordinary confinement as the INS ramped up its power to imprison. Attorney General John Ashcroft promised, "If you overstay your visa—even by one day—we will arrest you." Tens of thousands of people from predominantly Muslim countries were required to check in with immigration officials. Many were not allowed to walk out the same doors they had walked in. With the threat of terrorism sheathing law enforcement plans, a Muslim man accused of "anti-American statements"—which, in the words of a later Justice Department review, "were very general and did not involve threats of violence or suggest any direct connection to terrorism"—was among approximately 750 migrants detained for nothing more than allegedly violating immigration law.[31] They were held for long periods in INS facilities in Oakdale, Louisiana, and Miami; Bureau of Prisons sites in Kansas and New York; and county jails across New Jersey.

The most notorious feature of this episode was the harsh conditions inside the Metropolitan Detention Center, a maximum-security federal prison in Brooklyn. Inside the MDC, detainees were sent to a special high-security wing of the prison. These cells are designed for people deemed too dangerous to be anywhere near other prisoners; they are the most restrictive type of cell in the federal prison system. Though the "administrative maximum" special housing unit wasn't new, the September 11 detainees were sent there without the usual individualized review to determine dangerousness. No one bothered to ask whether these people should be in this place. Nonetheless, as the Justice Department's inspector general would disclose two years later, they "were subjected to the most restrictive conditions of confinement authorized by BOP policy, including 'lockdown' for 23 hours a day, restrictive escort procedures for all movement outside of the ADMAX SHU cells, and tight limits on the frequency and duration of legal telephone calls." For a time, the inspector general added, they were even subjected to a "communications blackout." When someone called to ask if one of the September 11 detainees was being held there, staff "often told people inquiring . . . that the detainee was not being held at MDC when, in fact, he was."[32] Swallowed by the force of immigration imprisonment, these people effectively disappeared from the face of the Earth.

Already enmeshed in public and private vehicles of wealth creation and lodged in the minds of elected officials as economic engines, immigration prisons are ripe for growth. The number of immigration prisoners held by the U.S. Marshals Service, ICE, and the Bureau of Prisons grows steadily. Even if it doesn't expand every year, it is unmistakably on an upward trajectory. By the time President Obama exited the White House in January 2017, the nation's immigration prison population had reached record levels. President Trump promised to build on that, and his early years in office suggested he was heading in that direction. ICE transitioned from the Obama era to the Trump era, surpassing its previous record high of 34,376 people detained on average every day, reached in fiscal year 2016, the last that fell completely within Obama's tenure. The following year—split about one-third under Obama

and two-thirds under Trump—the agency detained 38,106 people each day.[33] In the first year fully with Trump at the helm, ICE
confined 42,188 people daily.

Meanwhile, the legal authorization for more confinement
continues to get more expansive. In 2014, ICE's lawyers repeatedly told federal judges that they needed to detain women and
children to deter others from coming, despite established legal
principles that deterrence isn't a permissible justification for civil
detention; it's only a reason to punish people criminally. Recognizing that courts were unwilling to let the boundary between
civil and criminal confinement slip so easily beyond recognition,
DHS eventually shifted course by dropping its deterrence rationale. It did nothing to alter its practices, though. Instead, it found
more legally sound reasons to detain by claiming that the families
would disappear into the nation's interior or endanger the public.

Government officials remain creative in their attempts to lock
up more migrants. Federal prosecutors have successfully staved
off attempts to curtail special procedures that let them run migrants through criminal proceedings en masse. Judges oversee
dozens—as many as one hundred at times—of migrants at once
in hearings organized under Operation Streamline. The response,
a federal appeals court wrote, is "an indistinct murmur or medley
of yeses."[34] Brought to courthouses by U.S. Marshals, they are frequently shackled at the hands and feet in a display of "cattle call"
justice, one defense attorney said.[35]

Outside the federal courtrooms, officials have also confined
people inside stables built for cows, literally. On the morning of
May 12, 2008, roughly nine hundred law enforcement agents—
from local police to ICE officers—raided an enormous meatpack-
ing plant in Postville, Iowa. According to a press release issued
that day by federal prosecutors, "agents executed a criminal search
warrant . . . for evidence relating to aggravated identity theft,

fraudulent use of Social Security numbers and other crimes, as well as a civil search warrant for people illegally in the United States."

All told, they arrested almost four hundred migrants. Most were sent to the National Cattle Congress, a century-old fairground in nearby Waterloo where prized dairy cows are trotted. There, the arrested migrants were taken in groups of ten before a federal judge, who sat in a makeshift court more commonly known to Cattle Congress regulars as the "Electric Park Ballroom." Almost all would soon plead guilty to the federal crime of using false documents to work.[36] Ordinary workers had been turned into criminal aliens and shipped to a sixty-acre fairground built to show off stock animals. Erik Camayd-Freixas, a long-time interpreter who was present at the Cattle Congress court, recounted the experience he witnessed: "Driven single-file in groups of 10, shackled at the wrists, waist and ankles, chains dragging as they shuffled through, the slaughterhouse workers were brought in for arraignment . . . before marching out again to be bused to different county jails. . . . It is no longer enough to deport them: we first have to put them in chains."[37]

Today, almost two decades into the twenty-first century, imprisonment retains its central position in the nation's immigration law-enforcement apparatus, but it can no longer be said to operate independently of other areas of law. It is instead firmly entrenched in a broader securitization regime, in which the government uses brute force as evidence that it remains in control and that the nation remains sovereign. In turn, the twenty-first-century pursuit of security builds off the decades-long fetishization of imprisonment. The prison is a social service, a public good—even a humanitarian gesture. The United States could, in the traditional criminal-law context, kill people, or, in the immigration context, let migrants die in the desert. Instead, the federal government sends them to facilities that resemble "summer camp," long-time ICE official Matthew Albence told Congress in 2018, months before he would be promoted to the agency's second highest post.[38] That the United States chooses to imprison instead is a sign of graciousness: bare-knuckled, poisonous graciousness.

To the migrants locked up, most of whom come from Latin America, the prison walls are just a concrete reminder of their marginalized position within a global economic order that prizes the disposability of exploitable labor. Sociologist Tanya Golash-Boza calls this the "immigration industrial complex." With an obvious reference to President Eisenhower's famous lament about the federal government's increasing dependence on private corporations to provide national security, Golash-Boza describes a "convergence of interests" that lead to ever harsher immigration policies. Following the financial and political gains of immigration imprisonment allows us to see "who benefits from immigration law enforcement" and understand why it has become such an ingrained feature of twenty-first-century policing.[39]

Immigration imprisonment sets the modern marker of what the legal scholar Kevin Johnson calls the nation's "magic mirror." It lets us see our inner selves—what our worst demons would have us do to others even if we have a hard time admitting it to ourselves. It lets us glimpse the excesses to which we as a nation are willing to go when unconstrained by our better selves. How we might demonize our neighbors, fanning fear and destroying families. The immigration prison is a reminder that human bondage based on racial and economic markers of undesirability can't be relegated to some distant past. If we're willing to lock up people, we'll find a reason. Most of the time the targets will be people of color. We can call this a coincidence, but we would be lying to ourselves.

Part II

NOW

4

THE IMMIGRATION PRISON ARCHIPELAGO

From the outside, 200 Varick Street in Manhattan's Greenwich Village is unremarkable. Like other parts of the city's chic neighborhood, the street is noisy and congested. People race down the sidewalk, while the sounds of taxis and delivery trucks fill the air. Across the street, a Chipotle hands out burritos and expensive guacamole. Since 1929, the entire block between King Street and Houston Street has been occupied by a twelve-story office tower built in the art deco style that was popular at the time. The United States Appraisers' Stores Building, as it was originally known, was designed as a warehouse for imported merchandise seized by federal customs officials.[1] Its original name is long gone, and most people visiting the building in recent years are headed to the ground-floor post office. Above, the structure's warehousing roots are reflected in a different way. Instead of collecting goods shipped from abroad, the Varick Street building held migrants facing the prospect of removal from the United States. Instead of sorting mail, the employees sorted people.

Back in 1994, activists protesting outside read a letter written by Lulseged Dhine, at the time Varick Street's longest-serving prisoner. An Ethiopian Jew, Dhine fled his homeland in 1978 after his family was killed by the government because of their faith. But with a string of low-level drug crimes and a theft conviction on his record, all racked up since arriving in the United States,

he had become a "criminal alien" before the term became popular
with politicians. "His criminal history is very severe," an immigration judge wrote in denying the asylum application that Dhine
filed after the INS caught up with him while serving a one-year
prison term for cocaine possession. "The [federal government] is
not obliged to shelter people from despotic persecution abroad so
that they may enjoy lawful imprisonment in the United States," a
federal court wrote on appeal.[2] At Varick Street, Dhine had gone
four years without stepping foot outside. Still, he promised that,
if released, he would "leave all bitterness behind" and help other
prisoners. Two days later, he was moved to an Arizona prison "to
accommodate his request for fresh air and outdoor recreation," a
government spokesman said with vindictive irony. It would be another five years before Dhine found his freedom. And it was only
as recently as 2010, after years of public pressure, that the government moved its last prisoner out of Varick Street.[3]

Two thousand miles away, the private Eloy Detention Center pokes out of the Arizona desert, seemingly despite itself. "All
you see is dust," says Lauren Dasse, an Arizona native and lawyer
who has spent too many hours to count inside the Eloy prison.
Approaching Eloy after sunset, there is an otherworldly feel to
it. Bright lights blast through the kind of darkness that only the
desert brings. Driving there from the highway connecting Tucson
to Phoenix, for ten miles the towering cacti straddling the road
are all that keeps watch. To me, it looks like something out of
the X-Files. And when the wind picks up, clouds of dust sweep
through like Smoky Mountain fog.

There is nothing architecturally interesting about the Eloy facility. It consists of barbed wire surrounding a series of two-story
buildings: cell blocks and an immigration court, mostly. There is
nothing historically notable. It opened its doors in 1994 to house
immigration prisoners and hasn't stopped.[4] There are few people
available to notice its unremarkability. Like the prison, the town

of Eloy struggles to lift itself out of the desert's roughness. Off to the side of Phoenix and Tucson, its 16,000 residents include the 1,400 people locked inside the Hanna Road prison, almost all of whom would undoubtedly prefer not to be the town's imprisoned inhabitants.

Cut to the summer of 2014, when the number of people coming into the hands of Border Patrol agents was at a historical low and was continuing to drop steadily. In the midst of that lull, the number of children and families crossing the border jumped upward. So too did the reactions from pundits and politicians. Obama officials responded quickly and decisively with imprisonment as their chosen policy approach. Facing the reality that DHS was poorly equipped to house thousands of children and mothers, they opened a hastily planned detention center in Artesia, New Mexico, over three hours from El Paso to the southwest and Albuquerque to the northwest. Counting a mere 12,000 residents, Artesia is also home to the Federal Law Enforcement Training Centers (FLETC), a 1,300-acre complex that turns recruits into Border Patrol agents, training them in Spanish, constitutional law, and fence policing; according to its website, the FLETC includes "four International Border Fences replicating barriers used throughout various areas on the border between the United States and Mexico."[5]

Away from just about everything and everyone who wasn't already a federal agent or hoping to become one, Artesia's FLETC soon welcomed women and children requesting asylum in the United States. Behind two layers of barbed wire, they were housed inside corrugated metal trailers. Some had cribs. Interview rooms were bare bones: a few tables with uncomfortable chairs in a single room. Everyone could hear everyone else. Children were supposed to be occupied by a TV squeezed into a corner, while their mothers told stories of rape, beatings, and treacherous travels to the United States.

Thrown open with little time for planning, Artesia was a humanitarian failure. The mother of a six-year-old, who was detained there alongside her, recalls having too little food, water that made people sick, and long waits to see doctors. "The day-to-day conditions were horrible," she wrote anonymously in the *New York Times*. "It was no place for humans, let alone for families with small children."[6] As if to illustrate her point, a pair of medical experts hired by the government reported that staff had failed to spot a severely dehydrated infant even though the sixteen-month-old's mother had repeatedly taken the child to the prison's clinic. Despite the mother's efforts, doctors who lacked pediatric training sent her away, while the baby lost almost a third of his body weight.[7]

One of the first advocates to arrive in Artesia was a young attorney from Oregon, Julia Braker, who spent over $1,000 just to get to Artesia. Meeting with clients in a small space perversely called a "law library," which didn't include a single book or a computer that could access email, she nonetheless tried learning why migrants had come to the United States, searching for something that might become the basis of a legal claim to remain. All the while, she remembers, ICE guards were present, able to listen in on conversations about violence, rape, and gang intimidation.[8] There wasn't even a wall divider offering the superficial privacy of office cubicles. "I don't remember any guards ever blatantly listening in on conversations, but the room was small enough, and there were enough guards that they could overhear," she told me. Is it possible for people traumatized by violence and ignored by government officials—or worse—to confide their worst experiences under their jailer's watchful eyes? Perhaps, but it's not likely.

Two years later, Artesia, always imagined as a temporary facility, had been replaced by a couple of permanent family prisons in Texas, but problems remained. An advisory committee appointed by Obama's secretary of homeland security, Jeh Johnson, reported that the spaces available for attorney–client meetings at the South Texas Family Residential Center in Dilley and the Karnes County Residential Center in Karnes were "entirely insufficient for the number of detained individuals and the scope of legal issues to be addressed by families in detention." Rooms were so poorly designed that they "may even be prejudicial to ensuring effective communication and collaboration between attorneys and detainees."[9] Mothers fleeing sexual abuse were expected to describe their trauma in front of their children, even when their children were born of rape.[10] Children confined alone were expected to understand posters tacked on walls and designed for adults informing them that they had the right to meet with a lawyer.

These problems are so common across the immigration prison estate that a report by two advocacy groups described them as "endemic" to family detention.[11] The advocates meant to convey that these problems don't go away. Despite critique after critique, the same problems appear in one facility or another year after year. Indeed, the report's title echoes its criticism: "Locking Up Family Values, Again." The advocates are only partly correct. It is true that these problems don't go away. But in describing the problems as endemic to family detention centers, they suggest that the problems are separate from the facilities. The distinction between the problem of horrid conditions and the prisons themselves hints that reform is possible, if only people would start caring enough to do something about it.

Dora Schriro's description in her official report as a high-level DHS official was more accurate. ICE's detention system is designed to manage, control, stigmatize, and punish—all the goals of facilities "built . . . as jails and prisons to confine pre-trial and sentenced felons."[12]

Manhattan's Varick Street, Eloy's Hanna Road, and New Mexico's Artesia are evidence of just how different immigration prisons can be. There are county jails that sometimes are empty of people and government-owned facilities that house thousands. Some beds are tucked into urban neighborhoods; others are hidden along rural highways. Despite their vastly different appearances, they are joined by one central purpose: each of these facilities—and hundreds more—is prepared to imprison people who the government says violated immigration law.

Making sense of immigration imprisonment today requires understanding its sheer size. There is a lot to talk about, beginning with ICE, a division of the Department of Homeland Security, which runs the civil immigration detention system. Created in 2003 out of the Immigration and Naturalization Service, ICE has a $7.5 billion budget and twenty thousand law enforcement officers at its disposal. Most of that money—$4.2 billion in 2019— goes to its Enforcement and Removal Operations unit. When most people think of ICE, they're thinking of ERO. These are the SWAT team–style forces that bang on doors, demanding entry. In any given year, ICE detains somewhere in the vicinity of 400,000 people waiting to learn whether they will be allowed to remain in the United States.

Meanwhile, the federal criminal justice system also busies itself imprisoning migrants. Despite the frequent attention that the war on drugs receives for boosting the nation's prison population, the rising number of immigrant prisoners usually escapes notice. In the last years of the Obama administration, just shy of 100,000 people charged with a federal immigration crime were booked into the custody of the U.S. Marshals Service (USMS). They spent two to three months in jail simply waiting for their criminal case to be processed. In 2013, for example, marshals jailed 97,982 immigration-crime suspects. Every one of these people was charged with nothing worse than an immigration crime—usually entering the United States without the federal government's permission. In contrast, that same year the USMS took into custody 28,323 federal drug-crime defendants. People suspected of having committed a federal weapons crime trailed behind at 8,129, and those suspected of a violent offense at 4,511. To find a year in which immigration-crime prosecutions did not lead the most people into federal custody, we must go back to 2003, when immigration prosecutions came second only to drug prosecutions. Since then, it has skyrocketed, while everything else has flat-lined. The split is now so stark that it is hard to imagine it losing its top spot.

Just about everyone charged with a federal immigration crime is eventually convicted, and when that happens, migrants are usually sentenced to prison. Sometimes a judge gives them time served, a sentence that accounts for the nonviolent nature of illegal entry and reentry. Other times, they are sent to a federal penitentiary. Though they tend to receive shorter prison terms than people convicted of federal crimes overall, they are slightly more likely to be sentenced to prison time. On a given night, roughly 10 percent of the Bureau of Prisons population has been convicted of an immigration crime—something like 20,000 people per night.[13]

Like the federal government, many states use their incarceration power to target migrants for nothing more than their immigration status. Arizona infamously tapped its criminal justice system to raise the stakes of immigration-law violations when Governor Jan Brewer signed into law Senate Bill 1070 in 2010. Though the Supreme Court found major portions of that bill unconstitutional, it left intact the law's centerpiece: the "show me your papers" provision authorizing police officers to ask people about their immigration status. A wrong answer could open the doors into the immigration prison pipeline. S.B. 1070 certainly stands as Arizona's most publicized effort to penalize immigration-law violations, but it was not the first time that the state did so. Since the early 2000s, the state has repeatedly attempted to incarcerate migrants. In 2006, voters amended the state constitution to bar judges from releasing migrants suspected of certain crimes if police thought they had violated federal immigration law.

Arizona is most prominent among the states turning to their criminal justice systems to target immigration-law violations, but it's far from alone. S.B. 1070 spurred a series of copycat laws in Alabama, Georgia, and elsewhere. Missouri limits bail options, effectively jailing migrants, when United States citizens facing the same charges would be free. In Oklahoma, Florida, and Texas, it's a crime to help unauthorized migrants avoid immigration officers. In the spring of 2017, as the new Trump administration ratcheted up the rhetoric surrounding immigration, legislators in several states followed suit. In Colorado, a junior state senator hoped to force sheriffs' departments to lock up migrants anytime ICE requested it—even if that meant clashing with the Fourth Amendment. Though that proposal died in a Democratic-controlled committee, legislators in other states were more successful. In Texas, the state senate approved a bill penalizing cities that release people against whom ICE has issued an immigration detainer.

Immigration prisons are filled with an eclectic mix of inmates: teenagers fleeing forced conscription into gangs, mothers escaping abusive husbands with their children in tow, long-term permanent residents picked up because of a conviction, and unauthorized migrants who, for one reason or another, found themselves on the radar of a police officer whose department works hand-in-hand with ICE. Twenty-eight-year-old Selene Saavedra Roman, for instance, was a long-time U.S. resident with roots as deep as her years permitted, but her legal status was clouded. In the storied world of Texas football, no rivalry has higher stakes than match-ups between the University of Texas and Texas A&M. Saavedra Roman had clearly chosen her side. She was an Aggie married to an Aggie. Within a few years of graduating from A&M, she was flying high above Texas as a flight attendant for Mesa Airlines, a small company that runs flights for bigger fleets. By that time, she had patched over decades of living in the United States without authorization by taking advantage of Deferred Action for Childhood Arrivals (DACA), President Obama's highly controversial policy of pushing to the bottom of the government's priorities the deportation of hundreds of thousands of unauthorized migrants brought to the United States as children. Like other DACA beneficiaries, Saavedra Roman had a work permit. There was nothing out of order with her airline job. After a lifetime of being unable to travel, this dreamer, as unauthorized migrant youth are often called, had accomplished her dream.

Little did she know that a combination of governmental mean-spiritedness and employer incompetence would put her behind bars during the winter of 2019. Scheduled for a flight to Mexico, Saavedra Roman reminded her employer of her DACA status, but the company told her that she had nothing to worry about and that her return to the United States would be as seamless as everyone else's. But under Trump, targets had been set on DACA by the right, and ICE had started picking up people with DACA status as well as people who had applied for DACA, sending them into its prison network. In February 2019, Saavedra Roman would follow them there. When her flight landed, Customs and Border Protection officials at Houston's airport declared her an excluded Peruvian national. They probably would have deported her immediately except for her DACA status, but instead they sent her to an immigration prison in nearby Conroe. "I called, I texted, I screamed to the sky," her husband, David Watkins, said of the moment he learned she had been jailed. As a U.S. citizen, David had asked the federal government to issue his wife a green card. But the slog through the immigration process is slow, and by those pivotal days in early 2019, no answer had arrived except for the stark reality of the ICE prison. In Conroe, the young couple could see each other weekly—always divided by a thick glass window. It would take a public uproar and six weeks before she was released.[14]

Saavedra Roman and her husband went through an ordeal, but at least they were adults with years of living in the United States. In contrast, take a woman known in public court records simply as E.G.S., who was a newcomer to the United States. Originally from El Salvador, the thirty-five-year-old arrived in Texas after a weeks-long trek, fleeing from members of one of the world's most notorious gangs, MS-13. She had been raped on multiple occasions, and gang members had threatened to kill her. Along with her twelve-year-old daughter, E.G.S. sought asylum in the United States the only way possible under United States law—by coming to the United States in person. Anyone "who is physically present in the United States . . . irrespective of such alien's status, may apply for asylum," federal law provides.[15] Both violated immigration law in order to comply with asylum law. For this, mother and daughter were taken to the Karnes County Residential Center, a five-hundred-bed facility in Central Texas, one of three facilities dedicated to holding families. There, E.G.S. claimed in court records, her daughter was subjected to sexual harassment and assault by other detainees.[16]

Had the twelve-year-old arrived alone, she would have been handed over to the Office of Refugee Resettlement (ORR), a little-known corner of the Department of Health and Human Services that contracts almost exclusively with nonprofits to run "shelters" with electronic locks on the exterior doors and tall fencing along a perimeter that is constantly watched through surveillance cameras. In 2016, ORR housed about 60,000 kids. The number went down to 41,000 the following year and back up to 49,000 a year later, but this is still a dramatic increase from the 7,200 kids in ORR custody a decade earlier, in 2008.[17] In the summer of 2018, ORR's facilities, all of which are owned and operated by contractors, were thrust into the media spotlight when a Trump administration policy declared that it was best to separate families: detain and deport parents, while kids get shuttled into one of a hundred ORR facilities. Its largest partner, an Austin-based nonprofit named Southwest Key, runs about two dozen sites. In Brownsville, Texas, it uses an old Walmart. In Tucson, a converted motel.

Other migrants are imprisoned so that they can be punished. In the federal system, everyone convicted of a crime and sentenced to prison is handed over to the custody of the Bureau of Prisons (BOP). Migrants are no different. In the summer of 2019, the BOP operated ten "criminal alien requirement" prisons, which were exclusively reserved for migrants. Like in the rest of the federal prison system, there are a lot of drug offenders in these facilities, but about a third of inmates are there solely because they violated immigration law.[18] Instead of waiting to hear what an immigration judge or asylum officer has decided about their ability to stay in the United States, immigration offenders under the BOP's oversight have already been prosecuted and convicted of a federal crime. Almost always they plead guilty to entering the United States without authorization or doing that after a previous deportation.

Whether migrants are jailed as part of an immigration court case or as part of a criminal prosecution, sometimes the same facility is used. All that changes is the federal agency that pays the bills. The Cibola County Correctional Center in New Mexico went from housing convicted immigration offenders for the BOP to housing people ICE was trying to deport. Willacy County in Texas went in the opposite direction: from ICE to BOP prisoners.

In Cibola County and Willacy County, the same activity is being targeted, the same people are being locked up. Sometimes justified by civil legal powers given to ICE or U.S. Marshals, and at other times by criminal authority wielded by BOP, to the migrants who are under constant surveillance and whose liberty has been denied there is little difference. As an official government

report put it in 2009, "Immigration Detention and Criminal Incarceration detainees tend to be seen by the public as comparable,
and both confined populations are typically managed in similar
ways."[19] This similarity is not lost on detained migrants. In the
words of former ICE detainee Malik Ndaula, "They call immigration detention civil confinement, but prison is prison no matter
what label you use, and prison breaks people's souls, hearts, and
even minds."[20]

Labels do matter. Rhetoric is important. Just like it matters
that Presidents Obama and Trump claimed their immigration policing tactics made the country safer, what we call the sites where
migrants are confined is similarly consequential. DHS takes pains
to say they are "detention centers," "servicing processing centers," or "residential centers"—anything but jails or prisons. This
would be fine if there were a meaningful difference between an
ICE lockup and the typical county jail or state prison. Only there
isn't. Of the hundreds of facilities that ICE uses to confine migrants, many are county jails, without even the pretense of being
anything other than penal institutions that house people charged
with or convicted of crimes. They are owned by the county, operated by the sheriff, and built to keep inside the people arrested
every day in cities throughout the United States for a vast array of
crimes—anything from murder to underage drinking. ICE essentially rents beds from the county sheriff.

When it doesn't send migrants to county jails, it sends them to
other locations that look a lot like county jails. Entry and exit are
controlled, movements inside are tightly regulated, the perimeter
is laced with barbed wire, and security governs daily life. The same
holds true of facilities used by the U.S. Marshals and Bureau of
Prisons. Sometimes even the superficial change of switching federal government patron is too much. At the Otay Mesa Detention
Center south of San Diego, ICE and U.S. Marshals simply house
their immigration prisoners in the same prison at the same time.

All that's different is the color of their uniforms. What is called a prison or correctional institution when under contract with the USMS or BOP isn't magically transformed when ICE chooses the uniform color.

Writing on behalf of the majority of the Supreme Court, Justice Abe Fortas took a similar approach toward confinement facilities for young people. "A boy is charged with misconduct," he explained. "The boy is committed to an institution where he may be restrained of liberty for years. It is of no constitutional consequence—and of limited practical meaning—that the institution to which he is committed is called an Industrial School. The fact of the matter is that, however euphemistic the title, a 'receiving home' or an 'industrial school' for juveniles is an institution of confinement in which the child is incarcerated for a greater or lesser time. His world becomes 'a building with whitewashed walls, regimented routine and institutional hours.' Instead of mother and father and sisters and brothers and friends and classmates, his world is peopled by guards, custodians, state employees, and 'delinquents' confined with him for anything from waywardness to rape and homicide." [21]

Justice Fortas's point was quite simple: to the youth inside, it felt like a prison no matter what the sign above the door said. Likewise, to the people inside the confinement facilities used for those who have violated immigration law, they feel like prisons, whether operated by ICE, USMS, or BOP. Inmates are grouped into color-coded categories based on security classifications that dictate who can go where and when. Oranges can't be mixed with blues. Reds shouldn't be left unattended. In staff-strapped facilities, that sometimes means prisoners are stuck inside cell blocks when they're scheduled for court or the other way around: once a hearing is over, they are forced to sit in a courtroom waiting cell because facility rules say they can't be trusted to walk back to their dormitories. "It's pretty much like a regular jail," Army veteran

Gerardo "Jerry" Armijo said of the Port Isabel Detention Center after his stint there.

No matter the words plastered onto a sign outside, or who writes the checks that pay the staff, prisons have the same effect, with enormous costs. The human impact of incarceration is well-known. Detainees deal with the psychological toll of confinement, sometimes compounding the trauma that pushed them to leave the violence they have fled. Spouses struggle to keep families afloat, sometimes falling into homelessness. Local governments and charitable organizations frequently step into the fray. States provide housing assistance to family members, cities pay more for in-school support services, and charities offer food. One study found that 16 percent of migrants detained by ICE in Southern California who had families they supported financially reported problems paying rent or a mortgage prior to detention. After being taken into ICE's custody, that number jumped to 64 percent. Over one-third said their families couldn't pay for food, and four out of ten reported family difficulty paying for necessary medical care.[22]

ICE's enforcement tactics only augment the heavy weight of family separation. Instead of allowing parents to prepare children emotionally—or at least soften the blow—for a parent's forced removal, ICE frequently swoops into a family's life like a SWAT team. "In the pre-dawn hours of March 6, 2007, federal immigration officers pulled up in white vans in front of three large apartment buildings. Suddenly, without warning, agents identifying themselves as police stormed the building and began pounding on doors," elementary school principal Kathryn Gibney told Congress about the day in March 2007 when agents stretched through her students' Marin County, California, neighborhood. In a matter of minutes, children go from normalcy to living without a parent. "They handcuffed parents in front of their children and took them away, threatening that they would soon be back for others," she added.[23] It's as if a parent simply disappeared. Wrapping their minds around a parent's sudden departure proves too much for some. Depression frequently follows, with poor school performance close behind. Sometimes that morphs into destructive behaviors like self-cutting or drug abuse.[24]

Under strains like this, it's no wonder that families suffer. As one study of 132 migrants in New England found, the more vulnerable parents are to detention and deportation, the more their children feel the impact.[25] Children often end up struggling in school, responding with misbehavior and apathy toward classwork. That some manage to piece together a semblance of normalcy is mind-boggling. When the nightmare of family separation happens, migrants tap the power of what anthropologists call "familismo." Through the presumption that relatives and close friends form part of an extended family network, migrants can get financial and emotional support. One group of researchers studying mass arrests in Colorado, Massachusetts, and Nebraska found that "familismo was an effective response to the emergency needs of children," but even that came under strain after a few days or weeks.[26]

Cecilia Equihua knows that feeling. Her father's imprisonment came with a heavy burden on her. When she visited him in Florence, Arizona, near Eloy, she felt that she was also in prison. "I had never had the experience of seeing my dad behind a glass pane and having to talk to him through a phone," she told me. When he wound up in Cibola County, New Mexico, after an illegal reentry conviction months later, she decided to stick to letters.

We don't know precisely how many immigration prisoners have relatives in the United States, but it's a large number. From 1998 to 2007, the federal government deported 108,439 parents of U.S. citizen children, the DHS inspector general reported. On average, they had lived in the United States for ten years.[27] In one Arizona immigration prison, 86 percent of women reported having at least one U.S. citizen child, most of whom were under ten years old.[28] All of these kids are entitled to remain in the United States. Often, that's exactly what happens, even as a parent becomes a distant memory or little more than a face on a phone screen.

Criticism of immigration prisons is widespread but limited in scope. Journalists regularly disclose the prison system's unsavory truths. I often talk to reporters who have spent countless tedious hours sitting inside courtrooms and many more trying to get inside prisons. They talk to prisoners and family members. They tap the power of the Freedom of Information Act, the premier government transparency law in the United States. Likewise, advocates consistently lodge fiery rhetoric and litigation against prisons. They hold press conferences and convince superstars to hold concerts outside prison walls. They lobby elected officials. For their part, prisoners push back. They organize themselves, go on hunger strikes, and, at times, rebel forcefully.

Yet the immigration prison archipelago continues to thrive. It appears to be on autopilot. Its inevitability has been driven so firmly into conversations about a functioning immigration-law regime that even most migrants' advocates tend to assume that the United States has to lock up someone. The only real questions are who, how many, and under what conditions. Without doubt, those are important considerations. But they are also distractions. Rhetorical fights over what is best to use as a marker of undesirability misses the point that everything about drawing lines around some people—figuratively and literally—is rife with complications and unintended consequences. Fitting some people into cages is also unnecessary to ensure a functioning immigration-law system. As a policy, immigration imprisonment is a failure. As a legal principle, it is a sign of virtually unbridled executive power and an example of law's willingness to push migrants into a marginal, by-their-fingernails hold on to recognition inside court-rooms. As a measure of our collective morality, it's a humanitarian catastrophe. But as a sharp-edged political tool, it is a remarkably effective means of dividing workplaces, friendships, families, and communities.

5

THE GOOD IMMIGRANT VS.
THE BAD IMMIGRANT

David Rodriguez's star looked to be rising quickly. A celebrated chef at a trendy Houston cafe, Rodriguez's days mostly revolved around feeding what a review in a local newspaper described as "the cool kids" at "downtown's new 'it' spot."[1] Born in Mexico, Rodriguez came to the United States in 1997 when he was thirteen years old. Another thirteen years passed and, in 2010, he and his girlfriend, Vanessa, were heading home when two drunk men threatened her. Rodriguez pulled a bat out of the car and took a swing at the men, hitting them, before driving away. He later pled guilty to misdemeanor assault and moved on with his life and work. Years passed, and in 2015 Vanessa became his wife, and they decided on Belize for their honeymoon. They had no way of knowing that their days of paradise would give way to a family nightmare.

Rodriguez's professional success came to a screeching halt when he and Vanessa stepped off the airplane in Miami. Reviewing Rodriguez's background, an immigration officer at the airport concluded he was deportable. That five-year-old conviction, the Customs and Border Protection official thought, qualified as a crime involving moral turpitude, enough to land Rodriguez in prison. Those four words—"crime involving moral turpitude"— have been part of immigration law since 1891, and the phrase's meaning remains vague, ambiguous, and open to interpretation to this day. What was inherently base a century ago might not be today.

Even today, federal law tells government officials to use "the moral standards generally prevailing in the United States."[2] Yet officials are given broad discretion, especially in fast-acting situations like the airport screenings, where Rodriguez came under scrutiny. As far as the law goes about assault, simple assault isn't a crime involving moral turpitude, but other types of assault are. Because there is so little consistency about what legally constitutes moral turpitude, it shouldn't come as a surprise that a border official thought Rodriguez's crime fit the bill. How is someone who isn't a lawyer and receives limited training on the inner workings of immigration law supposed to track the meaning of this term? The words of one congressman, said a century ago as he tried to get the phrase out of immigration law, ring true today: "No one can really say what is meant by saying a crime involving moral turpitude."[3]

It might be hard to know what qualifies as a crime involving moral turpitude, but it matters. If the border official were correct, Rodriguez could be kicked out of the country. If wrong, he could go back to his life of creating critically acclaimed meals for Houston's trendsetters. But for the long-time resident with deep ties to the booming Texas metropolis, the possibility of not getting to live in the United States wasn't the only tough reality. The airport immigration officer's accusation of debased conduct meant he would have to fight the government's immigration charges from inside prison. That is exactly what happened. From inside a private immigration prison in Houston, Rodriguez watched Thanksgiving, Christmas, and New Year's Day pass. "You're nowhere, and you're somewhere," he mused when I spoke with him inside his current business success: a "creative lifestyle destination" selling shoes, books, art, and espresso. He shared that limbo space in detention with a rotating bunch of over three dozen men. After seventy-eight days, he was released when an immigration judge decided that the conviction did not make him removable.[4]

No one would claim that David Rodriguez is perfect, but looking only at his actions, disconnected from everything else, ignores key details. The men he hit threatened his future wife. Removed from the encounter that night, it's easy to say that Rodriguez was in the wrong. Even if that's correct, the rest of his life suggests that this moment of violence was the exception. Far more common is the cool-headed Rodriguez that prevails in the high-pace, heated environment of restaurant kitchens.

If we consider Rodriguez's life as a whole, it becomes easier to excuse his actions. Indeed, when a prosecutor got involved in his criminal case years before he wound up in ICE's clutch, something like that happened. He was first charged with a felony. After the prosecutor learned more about what happened, he agreed that a felony charge was too serious. Instead, Rodriguez and the prosecutor agreed to the reduced misdemeanor offense he pled guilty to. Had the prosecutor focused only on Rodriguez's actions, he would have just focused on the brutality of taking a baseball bat to another person. Criminal law is more sophisticated than that. It accounts for the basic fact that actions happen in a particular context. On that night when Rodriguez and Vanessa were making their way home, only to be accosted, context mattered.

In the United States, exceptionalism is baked into our collective mythology. We think of ourselves as special people who have created a uniquely extraordinary country. The story of the nation's birth does not involve Roman gods or Greek epics, but it does involve an equally preposterous myth of selfless, hard-working, God-fearing intrepid spirits. The colonial "city upon a hill," as John Winthrop put it in 1630, has come to symbolize the settler community's desire to stand watch over the ostensibly barren wilderness where nature's bounty waited to be exploited and barbarian tribes had to be extinguished. Winthrop's sermon actually gave his followers some leeway, but the part that has become ingrained in national culture isn't so forgiving. On the contrary, the colonial myth of exceptionalism appears centuries later in the work of people who shared little in common with Winthrop's puritanism. Writing in 1859, the abolitionist and author of *Uncle Tom's Cabin*, Harriet Beecher Stowe, wrote that "in no other country were the soul and the spiritual life ever such intense realities" as in New England.[5]

Four centuries after Winthrop's speech off the coast of what would become New England, grandiosity governs our political culture. Occasionally, politicians invoke Winthrop explicitly, like when Ronald Reagan quoted the "city upon a hill" line the night before election day in 1980.[6] Two terms later, he turned to Winthrop again, explaining that, when he envisioned Winthrop's fairytale city, "in my mind it was a tall, proud city built on rocks stronger than oceans, windswept, God-blessed, and teeming with people of all kinds living in harmony and peace; a city with free ports that hummed with commerce and creativity. And if there had to be city walls, the walls had doors and the doors were open to anyone with the will and the heart to get here."[7]

Most of the time, though, U.S. exceptionalism manifests itself in more subtle forms. In a memorable speech marking fifty years since police violently beat civil rights advocates in Selma, Alabama, Barack Obama described the "American instinct" as "the idea held by generations of citizens who believed that America is a constant work in progress; who believed that loving this country requires more than singing its praises or avoiding uncomfortable truths. It requires the occasional disruption, the willingness to speak out for what is right, to shake up the status quo. That's America. That's what makes us unique."[8]

So fully immersed in the United States' psyche that presidents as starkly different as Reagan and Obama incorporate the idea into major speeches, exceptionalism has also become ingrained in the law that determines who is fit for membership in the political community: immigration law. Like a bouncer at a trendy nightclub, immigration law demands superficial extraordinariness. For most of the nation's history, voluntarily migrating to the United States meant being white. Explicit racial restrictions are now a thing of the past, but the promise that the United States welcomes "anyone with the will and the heart to get here" is flat out false.

Migrants are expected to live out the exceptionalism that U.S. citizens imagine in themselves. Since 1965, immigration law has been structured around two narrow guiding principles: people can come to the United States to reunite with certain family members already here or to contribute to industries in need of high-skill workers. As a result, successfully navigating the immigration process generally requires having the right family ties or the right job. If you do not, you are pretty much assured you won't be granted permission to take up residence in the United States. Obtaining either of these requires some effort and a lot of luck. Having a relative in the United States who can request that you join them generally turns on who your parents are or who you marry. Getting the right job depends on going to the right schools, pursuing the right degree plan, navigating the right job prospects in just the right way—and making sure that there are not too many people in the United States doing that too. Most of these hinge on what opportunities parents provide their children—a fact completely beyond any individual's control.

It also hinges on wealth. The United States is notorious among wealthy nations for stomaching enormous inequality. Executives earn 312 times as much as their employees.[9] Almost one out of five children lives in poverty.[10] Walk through any major city and the homeless population is a reminder that many people do not have a roof over their heads. Yet immigration law expects much more. People can't get visas if they might become a "public charge," a hard-to-pin metric that requires a family-member sponsor to prove that they can feed an extra mouth and stay above 125 percent of the federal poverty level. In 2018, the Trump administration even floated a proposal to deny visas to people who had received a government subsidy to buy prescription medication insurance through Medicare.

Once they have made it to the United States, migrants are again held to a higher standard than U.S. citizens are. Migrants caught up in just about any criminal activity are in peril. From the unauthorized migrant caught driving without a license to the permanent resident convicted of possessing a single joint of marijuana, federal law permits government officials to detain and potentially remove people who flout a wide variety of run-of-the-mill criminal laws. Drop below the 125 percent threshold and you violate the terms of your stay. A woman who obtains a green card because she married a U.S. citizen who then turned out to abuse her risks her legal status if they divorce. There is a legal route around this, but that requires a lawyer. Any of these people can be imprisoned while they try to resolve their immigration predicament.

In Colorado, where I live a few blocks from the closest marijuana dispensary, a U.S. citizen can buy twenty-eight grams of marijuana daily under a neon green cross, but for possessing anything more than thirty grams a noncitizen can wind up in ICE custody.[11] The most charitable avenue for avoiding the harsh confinement and removal of today's immigration policing practices—a device called cancellation of removal—is off-limits to people convicted of any of the twenty-one types of crimes called aggravated felonies.

Pursuing aggravated felony claims, sometimes the government goes too far, even for the courts. Obama administration lawyers took a case to the Supreme Court involving a man caught with one Xanax pill. He was convicted of simple possession, a misdemeanor, and got ten days in a Texas jail. To the federal government, this was a drug-trafficking crime that left ICE no choice but to lock up José Ángel Carachuri-Rosendo while an immigration judge decided whether he would be deported. The Court disagreed.[12]

A few years later, Obama administration lawyers were back at the Supreme Court arguing that a sock Moones Mellouli was wearing was a form of drug paraphernalia. Inside it, Mr. Mellouli had stuffed four tablets of Adderall, the common attention deficit hyperactivity disorder medication, but Justice Department lawyers did not focus on the medication. Instead, they claimed the sock was enough to win the aggravated felon label and, with it, warrant forced confinement and removal. Again, the Supreme Court disagreed, explaining that federal law does not criminalize "ready-to-wear items like socks," so it can't form the basis of immigration imprisonment and removal.[13]

It hasn't always been this way. For most of U.S. history, second chances were built into immigration law. Most of the time, crime was irrelevant to a person's ability to make a life here. Neither imprisonment nor removal were part of the calculations most migrants made. In most instances, federal law did not authorize imprisonment specifically for migrants. People who were suspected or convicted of a crime were locked up on the same terms whether they were U.S. citizens or not. Starting in the 1980s, sea changes swept immigration law. "While once there was only a narrow class of deportable offenses and judges wielded broad discretionary authority to prevent deportation," the Supreme Court wrote in a landmark 2010 decision, *Padilla v. Kentucky*, "immigration reforms over time have expanded the class of deportable offenses and limited the authority of judges to alleviate the harsh consequences of deportation. The 'drastic measure' of deportation or removal is now virtually inevitable for a vast number of noncitizens convicted of crimes."[14]

Even the language that immigration law uses to describe

migrants evokes exceptionalism. To immigration lawyers and judges, there are no migrants. There are only citizens and "aliens," as if Hollywood scriptwriters took over for Congress. Everyone who doesn't fall into one category falls into the other. An alien, the Immigration and Nationality Act says, is "any person not a citizen or national of the United States." On the big screen, aliens are the unknown threat that arrives from a distant planet possessed of special capacities and advanced technologies. The language of immigration law conjures up a similar threat. Central Americans walking to the United States with backpacks and children in tow are "an invasion . . . and our Military is waiting," President Trump declared in late October 2018.[15] With an eerie similarity, Bill Pullman, playing president in the 1996 alien-invasion blockbuster *Independence Day*, rallied resistance forces "fighting for our freedom . . . from annihilation." Like their counterparts from outer space, human aliens from other countries are unknown, potentially dangerous, and superhuman.

Nonetheless, as if in response to the high demands placed on them, migrants tend to rise to the challenge. They are an exceptional lot. Migrants commit less crime than do people born in the United States. They are better educated. They are more religious. Through unions, faith groups, and community organizations, they involve themselves in civic life more than U.S. citizens do. But within this extraordinary bunch, there are plenty of normal, imperfect people. Some do commit crimes, from the most trivial to the worst acts imaginable. Some never had a chance to go to school; others didn't care to keep going. Plenty stay home on Sundays and live in relative solitude. Like U.S. citizens, migrants are a mixed bag. My mother finished the third grade but goes to church six or seven days a week. I am a lawyer and law professor, but I make it to church once every six or seven months (usually when visiting my mom). Regardless of their immigration status, humans are complicated, inherently imperfect, and often contradictory beasts. We don't fit neatly into boxes marked "good" or "bad."

Regrettably, much of the rhetoric that dominates political debate on immigration law misses this basic point. In a prime-time immigration speech on November 20, 2014, President Obama explained that his administration's immigration enforcement priorities target "felons, not families. Criminals, not children. Gang members, not a mom who's working hard to provide for her kids." President Obama's exhortation is as good an example as President Trump's trite comment about targeting "bad hombres." Both simplify complex human beings. Felons are part of families, just like one person's bad hombre might be another's father. "It hurts that he was trying to be a dad and he can't," Cecilia Equihua said about her father, locked up for returning to the United States to reunite with his kids. The easy sound bites make for politically useful talking points, but they are a lousy basis for public policy.

The shifting sands of the political debate about which migrants deserve to live freely in the United States and which don't expose the pernicious edge of sorting the good from the bad. Listen to most elected officials talk about immigration, and one commonality quickly becomes obvious. Everyone, it seems, wants to lock up and deport criminals. President Clinton signed laws that made it easier to land in an immigration prison and harder to get out. His successor, President Bush, inaugurated the era of hardline criminal prosecution of immigration-law violators. President Obama and his top immigration officials repeatedly claimed to focus their resources on so-called criminal aliens, and oversaw the largest immigration prison population in history until then. The Trump administration is no different. In his first week as president, Donald Trump signed an executive order declaring "aliens who engage in criminal conduct in the United States" to be a particularly "significant threat to national security and public safety."

Despite the consistent bipartisanship of tarring migrants who have committed a crime, it's impossible to sort the good from the bad consistently. Obama's "felons, not families" remark categorized people into two boxes: family members on the one hand and criminals on the other. Trump uses two different categories: law-abiding citizens, almost always depicted as white, and lawbreaking migrants, almost exclusively not white. Both categories are convenient rhetorical ploys that make for good sound bites, but neither can be defended logically. The criminals that Obama derided are also family members. Families include criminals, and criminals have families. Lots of crime, in fact, is committed against family members.

Politicians and pundits inclined to dislike migrants have a sharp eye for their worst mistakes. When Iowa police pinned blame for the murder of white college student Mollie Tibbets on Cristhian Bahena Rivera, an unauthorized migrant from Mexico, Trump quickly stood in front of a camera and complained, "We have tremendous crime trying to come through the border."[16] In Trump's view, crimes, not people, cross the border. By contrast, President Obama was the opposite of Trump's crudeness and callousness. Still, the Obama administration heavily publicized its policy of targeting migrants with criminal histories while going easy on people who had avoided blemishes. Even the DACA program was off-limits to young people who had been convicted of some crimes.

Trump's complaint is certainly cruder than the Obama administration's policy, but both examples fit into a broader bipartisan pattern. In political conversations, migrants are expected to be innocent. If they are not, they stop being in the good graces of policymakers—and the laws they make. "We love our victims innocent," writes the philosopher Mladen Dolar. "We empathize with them as long as they appear to be innocent, but the moment they display some trait that is not entirely amiable . . . the sympathy is cut short."[17] For U.S. citizens, blemishes are to be expected because humans are imperfect creatures. We mess up. President Trump expressed support for his campaign chairman Paul Manafort, who admitted to lying to the FBI. He pardoned his supporter Joe Arpaio, who was convicted of disobeying court orders. But he regularly harps on about the dangers migrants pose. In regards to the aliens who migrate to the United States, blemishes are red flags of which citizens should be wary.

In the United States of the late twentieth and early twenty-first centuries, to be wary is to be worried, and prisons are considered a suitable tactic to deal with our fears. Officially, the United States uses immigration prisons mostly to avoid crime and ensure that migrants appear for court dates. Neither justification stands up to close scrutiny. Migrants commit relatively little crime. Locking up hundreds of thousands of men, women, and children because someone, somewhere, at some time, might do something is ludicrous. Mostly, migrants end up behind bars because of overblown fears that they are violent predators on the loose. In the dispassionate description of legal scholar Emily Ryo, "concerns about immigrant criminality predominate immigration bond hearings," legal proceedings in which a migrant can ask an immigration judge for release from confinement.[18] Comments by Presidents Obama and Trump illustrate Ryo's point. In a 2012 debate against Republican presidential contender Mitt Romney, President Obama called some migrants "gangbangers."[19] President Trump harps on about gory beheadings. Within days of entering the White House, President Trump prioritized going after any migrant charged with a crime, even if no conviction resulted. A few months later, his attorney general, Jeff Sessions, claimed that "criminal aliens . . . seek to overthrow our system of lawful immigration."[20] Both administrations claim that they are going after the worst of the worst but disagree about where to draw that distinction.

Prisons are ingrained in the perception of a functioning immigration-law system in part because they are imagined as requirements of public safety. If the United States is to be protected from internal and external threats, the federal government must know who is inside the country and who is asking to enter. A political spat that developed in the midst of budget battles between the Obama White House and the Republican-led House of Representatives in 2013 illustrates just how deeply ingrained the assumption is that immigration prisoners pose a risk. That year, ICE announced that it would soon release several hundred detainees weekly from a population of almost 34,000. Over a three-week period, ICE released 2,228 people.[21] Without any information about whom ICE had in mind for release, the Speaker of the House of Representatives at the time, John Boehner, accused the agency of "letting criminals go free." His Republican colleague, the chair of the House Judiciary Committee, Bob Goodlatte, added, "Irresponsible decisions to release detained illegal immigrants unreasonably and unnecessarily put the public at risk."[22] Like Boehner, Goodlatte also didn't claim to know anything about the specific people on ICE's release list. Nonetheless, both immediately concluded that ICE's actions endangered the public.

Considering government-held information about whom it confines, Boehner's and Goodlatte's knee-jerk reactions are unfounded. ICE's prison population includes many people who have never been convicted of a crime. Adalberto Díaz Labrada came here from Cuba in search of asylum. For lacking the government's permission to arrive, he wound up at the Port Isabel Detention Center, the sprawling South Texas immigration prison tucked into picturesque brushland. In Port Isabel, "I was a number for twenty-one days," he told me when we spoke inside the busy bakery in Salt Lake City that he now runs. Appearances on the Food Network and a National Pastry Chef of the Year Award from the

American Culinary Federation have made him into a croissant celebrity—and with good reason. He is a baker and an artist.

The bakery is tucked neatly into a neighborhood full of low-slung, working-class homes, where businesses, customers, and employees go back-and-forth between English and Spanish. From this fragrant outpost, Díaz Labrada has embraced the political side of baking. To him, the bakery isn't just where people buy croissants; it's a space in which people from across his community can come together over a common interest. It's like he sees the pastry shop the same way many people see a church, rather than how the pastry-chef medals hanging along the shop walls suggest: a lone baker, seemingly isolated from everyone else.

When news broke in 2018 that children were being taken from their parents and shipped to immigration prisons, Díaz Labrada was shaken to act. Fifteen hundred miles from Port Isabel, he couldn't rush to the scene, but he could bake. Eighteen years after his own release from an immigration prison, he organized a bake sale that brought in $15,000 in donations to the Texas Civil Rights Project, the civil rights group that first exposed the Trump administration's family separation policy. "This is my power," he said. Not everyone wants to hear his message, but that's okay with him. "I was afraid and worried when I was twenty-eight" and held at Port Isabel, he said, before quickly adding, "but what would my reaction be if I was ten?"

Jakelin Caal would have liked to have known, too. Born in Guatemala in 2011, she was seven years old when she died inside a Border Patrol holding facility in December 2018, about forty-eight hours after entering the United States. The cause of death appears to have been sepsis, a treatable illness that sometimes hits people with vulnerable immune systems when their bodies are trying to ward off an infection. Anxious to turn the tables of blame, DHS announced her death while warning of the dangers of migrating to the United States. "Once again, we are begging parents to not put themselves or their children at risk by attempting to enter illegally," DHS wrote on its Facebook page.[23]

Less than three weeks later, Felipe Gómez-Alonzo made it to Christmas Eve, but no further. Eight years old, he also died in Border Patrol custody. His sister said that Felipe's dream was to study in the United States, then return to his family in Guatemala. Instead, he returned in a miniature coffin. "Because we're poor, we have to pass through things like this," his mother told a reporter a few months later.[24]

Even among people who do have a criminal record, many have been convicted of nothing that could be said to threaten public safety. Akio and Fusako Kawashima, for example, are "aggravated felons" in immigration-law parlance. They were both convicted of crimes that subjected them to mandatory detention while they fought their immigration cases and, after losing, as they awaited deportation to their native Japan. Their crimes? Tax fraud. Owners of Japanese restaurants in the Los Angeles area, Akio Kawashima filed a false federal corporate tax return. His wife, Fusako, helped. Both pled guilty and received a sentence of a mere four months in jail.[25] By the time of ICE's 2013 announcement of a pending detention center release, the Kawashimas had lost their legal challenges, even a battle in the Supreme Court, so they were not among ICE's detainees. Had they been, their release couldn't reasonably have been said to endanger anyone. Indeed, losing meant they were returned to Japan. Is Japan less safe than it was while this couple, fast approaching sixty years old, was running restaurants in California?

Boehner's and Goodlatte's reactions were extreme but not unusual. When a man who'd done numerous stints inside immigration prisons for removal proceedings and immigration crime convictions was accused of killing a young woman walking on a San Francisco pier with her father, Republican congressman Steve

King claimed that "Kate [Steinle's] beautiful life was taken from her . . . when she was shot in the back by an illegal alien who had previously been deported five times and was seeking refuge in a so-called 'sanctuary city.'"[26] Kate's Law, a bill Goodlatte introduced with King's co-sponsorship, made it through the House before stalling in the Senate. The bill would have massively expanded prison time for immigration crime offenses.[27]

As a candidate, President Trump declared his support for the law "in honor of the beautiful Kate Steinle who was gunned down in SF by an illegal immigrant" and repeatedly mentioned her by name.[28] The following summer, with the Republican Party's nomination in hand, he said in his acceptance speech at the Republican National Convention, "Of all my travels in this country, nothing has affected me more deeply than the time I have spent with the mothers and fathers who have lost their children to violence spilling across our border. . . . My opponent will never meet with them, or share in their pain. Instead, my opponent wants Sanctuary Cities. But where was sanctuary for Kate Steinle? . . . Where was sanctuary for all the other Americans who have been so brutally murdered, and who have suffered so horribly?"[29]

These examples aren't limited to Republicans. None other than liberal champion and long-time U.S. senator Dianne Feinstein pointed the finger at the San Francisco Sheriff's Department. The influential Democrat put the blame for Kate Steinle's "tragic killing" by José Inés García Zarate on San Francisco's refusal to abide by an ICE detainer request. According to a host of courts, the problem is that keeping someone behind bars simply at ICE's behest violates the Fourth Amendment. "I strongly believe that an undocumented individual, convicted of multiple felonies and with a detainer request from ICE, should not have been released," Feinstein said in an official statement. In a letter to San Francisco's mayor, she added, "The tragic death of Ms. Steinle could have been avoided if the Sheriff's Department had notified ICE prior to the release of Mr. Sanchez, which would have allowed ICE to remove him from the country," referring to García Zarate by an alias used in early reports. She urged the mayor to collaborate with ICE by holding people at ICE's request and joining an ICE initiative to identify and arrest people jailed by the city.[30]

Yet, despite being tarred by Trump, a jury found García Zarate not guilty. It turns out the jury was not convinced that he had set out to shoot Steinle. Instead, it appears that he found the gun on the sidewalk and accidentally set it off. No one knows who put it there, only that the gun had previously been left unattended in a vehicle belonging to a federal park ranger. Gun deaths are anything but unusual in the United States. From Charleston to Pittsburgh, we can point to real shots fired against people worshipping in the closest thing we've ever had to actual sanctuaries—our churches and synagogues. Painting García Zarate as a deranged demon pretends that gun deaths are uncommon and that Steinle's death resulted from García Zarate's depravity rather than from her bad luck in a gun-saturated environment.

For generations, public safety has been used as a justification for immigration imprisonment. When Ellen Knauff was trying to reunite with her World War II–veteran husband in the United States, immigration authorities confined her on Ellis Island. To immigration officials, her presence in the United States "would be prejudicial to the interests of the United States"—so much, in fact, that they refused even to give her a hearing at which she might learn the reason for her confinement and exclusion from the country whose war aims she had supported in Europe. "As all other aliens, petitioner had to stand the test of security," the Supreme Court explained while denying her claims. "This she failed to meet."[31] In his strident dissent, Justice Robert Jackson responded, "The plea that evidence of guilt must be secret is abhorrent to free men, because it provides a cloak for the malevolent, the misinformed, the meddlesome, and the corrupt to play the role of informer undetected and uncorrected."[32] Proving Jackson's point, years later Knauff won her freedom after an immigration court concluded she had been held on nothing more than rumors.

Ironically, imprisonment is even justified on humanitarian grounds. In the same year that the Supreme Court decided Knauff's case, immigration officials busied themselves excluding and detaining Ignatz Mezei. Like Knauff, Mezei was also kept on Ellis Island based on secret evidence of the security risk he presented. Again, the Court found no problem with this, even though Mezei was returning from an effort to visit his dying mother after twenty-five years of living in the United States.[33] Mezei, the Supreme Court concluded, was provided "temporary harborage" on Ellis Island, "a legislative grace."[34] More recently, DHS set up "family residential centers"—secured facilities in remote locations to which access is highly regulated—to protect mothers detained alongside their children. At the largest such facility cells are "bedroom blocks," and the facility is organized into "neighborhoods" named after brown bears, green turtles, and, as one lawyer put it, other "really cute names."[35] Couching confinement as a lifesaving example of graciousness allows officials involved in the detention process to feel upstanding but does nothing to lessen the harshness of the detention experience.

Touted as a humanitarian gesture that is nonetheless a public safety imperative, immigration imprisonment seems like the best of both worlds. Some migrants need protection; others we need protection from. Either way, imprisonment is good for the migrants who are locked up, and it's good for the rest of us who aren't. Rough spots exist, but they are imagined as the unruly edges of an otherwise upstanding policy. The violence that necessarily accompanies the prison experience is overlooked, and the fact that imprisonment should not even be on the table as a reasonable policy option isn't considered.

More than simply unjustified by safety concerns, like with other types of punishment, immigration imprisonment is dispatched in a manner that is racially biased. Twice over, actually. First, as Michelle Alexander and others have explained in great detail, the criminal justice system marks people as criminals through the well-known prisms of race and class. Poor people of color are policed, prosecuted, and punished more than are white people who engage in comparable misconduct. In the impoverished corner of South Texas in which I grew up, cops could show up at any moment. Border Patrol agents lurked outside stores downtown and drove along isolated roads near the Rio Grande. Every time I crossed the bridge back into Texas, I had to prove my right to be there and shed any suspicion that I was up to no good.

Then came college. During my first week in the Ivy League, I saw more crime than I ever had before. Marijuana came out from behind classics of English literature, and fake IDs were as common as late-night pizza. Had they wanted to, campus cops literally could have smelled their way to federal drug crimes. Once there, they probably would have found some underage drinking and identity theft. But they did not want to. As spaces that are dominated by wealthy white people, colleges are relatively privileged. City cops and campus law enforcement officers have little interest in cracking down on illegal activity perpetrated by the children of parents all too ready to use whatever influence they have to ensure that their children are able to learn who they are without the stigma of criminality attaching itself to them. That's a luxury many people of color do not have.

Immigration law piles on top of criminal law, becoming a second layer of racially biased punishment. The mandatory-detention provision of civil immigration law that requires ICE to take certain people into custody and that prevents immigration judges from letting them free turns almost exclusively on criminal activity.[36] On the criminal end of the immigration-law spectrum, migrants convicted of illegal reentry, a felony under federal law, are subject to much more prison time if they have prior convictions for certain offenses—from an eight-year bump following any felony conviction to an eighteen-year bump following an aggravated felony conviction.[37]

Policies promoted by both Democrats and Republicans reveal a critical reliance on the criminal justice system. Lock-step use of the criminal justice system to identify people who merit removal from the United States ignores its biases. Take, for example, the rate of imprisonment for black migrants. Often overlooked, there are roughly 3.7 million black migrants in the United States. This is about 7 percent of the total noncitizen population.[38] Reflecting the racially skewed criminal justice system, black migrants are more likely to be detained by ICE for a criminal reason than are other migrants. According to an analysis of 2014 immigration-court data, 14 percent of all migrants detained faced removal on a criminal basis. For black migrants, that number was closer to 50 percent. Not surprising, black migrants also make up an outsized percentage of the people detained by ICE because of a criminal ground for removal. In 2014, they made up 17 percent of migrants detained because of a crime, though they were less than 5 percent of the people facing the possibility of removal that year.[39]

Despite the lopsided racial impact, policymakers seldom question immigration imprisonment's use of the stigma of criminality. On the contrary, legislators have repeatedly endorsed greater entanglement between criminal law and immigration law, allowing the immigration-prison regime to grow into a sprawling prison archipelago. It should sit uncomfortably with policymakers that immigration law uses encounters with the criminal justice system to determine who is fit for imprisonment and removal.

Likewise, Trump's claim that migrants violate immigration law varies between misinformed and blatantly false.

Asylum-seekers who come to the United States without the federal government's permission certainly violate one aspect of immigration law, but they are also complying with the letter and spirit of another section. To jail asylum-seekers because they violated immigration law tramples on Congress's directive that anyone "who is physically present in the United States or who arrives in the United States (whether or not at a designated port of arrival . . .), irrespective of such alien's status" can request protection in the United States, a right echoed in international treaties.[40]

Counterintuitively, there is something refreshing about Trump's excesses. Instead of relying on the tragically biased criminal justice system to sort migrants into desirable and undesirable categories, Trump's approach doesn't turn on the effects of biased policing. Everyone falls into his net simply because they are aliens, tarred with the stigma of dangerousness, marked by the stain of race.

Even if we could agree on who is good and who is bad, using immigration law to sort migrants means that some people are targeted merely because they happened to be born on the wrong side of the border. Is my moral claim to belonging in the United States really so flimsy that it turns on the fact that my mother gave birth to me eight miles north of the Rio Grande rather than eight miles south? I like to think that it has more to do with the friends I've made here, the work I do with community groups, or the positive impact I have on students. Every day, I'm grateful for the opportunity I had to go to college. I don't regret for a second turning down all the offers I received from military recruiters when I was a high school student contemplating my next step in life. But does my good fortune mean my moral claim is stronger than that of Jerry Armijo, the man who was willing to sacrifice his life in service to this country? Is it stronger than that of Edgar Baltazar García, the

Army veteran with PTSD and a brain injury who was detained after an hours-long trip to Mexico?

Whether we categorize migrants as good or bad based on Obama's metrics or Trump's, we are still segregating based on nothing more than citizenship status, which has nothing to do with our individual contributions to the United States and even less to do with moral worth. Jerry Armijo and Edgar Baltazar García remind us that the legal chasm that divides citizens from everyone else leaves immigration imprisonment to fall on some and not on others because of politics, not morality. I don't have a moral claim to belonging in the United States that they don't. All I have that they don't is a U.S. passport. To me, that's not good enough.

The story of immigration imprisonment isn't a morality tale. Conversations about migrants are frequently divorced from reality, but that doesn't make them stories about right and wrong. President Trump's wife, Melania, who was born in Slovenia, once said that some people follow immigration law because that's just how they are. "It never crossed my mind to stay here without papers," she said in 2015 when her husband was still nothing more than an outlandish presidential contender. "That is just the person you are. You follow the rules. You follow the law."[41] To Melania, doing what immigration law requires is just a question of morals. Some people, like her, have it. Others don't.

I remembered that when I was living in Slovenia I experienced my own migration problems. There to do research supported by the State Department's Fulbright scholarship program, I had direct access to helpful officials at the United States Embassy. Even in the privileged situation that I was in, with a level of assistance unimaginable to most migrants (I once got wind that my predicament had made it to the ambassador's desk), I was close to going beyond the number of days I could be in Slovenia without a residence permit. But when I raised this with my embassy liaison, she responded assuredly, "Don't worry. If that happens, it won't be because you did anything wrong." That was small comfort, though it does make me laugh anytime I mention the story to immigration lawyers in the United States. Imagine telling a judge: "Yes, my client violated immigration law, but it wasn't his fault." That wouldn't help anyone escape handcuffs.

Melania is far from the only person to claim that people who violate immigration law are morally suspect, but her trite comment is a convenient reminder that migration can't be boiled down to morals. People don't move because they are innately ethical or unethical. They don't violate immigration restrictions for those reasons either, so they shouldn't be locked up for those reasons.

Years ago, I wrapped up a meeting with a client inside Willacy. Like many facilities, Willacy didn't have dedicated areas for lawyers to speak with clients privately. In the rush to build the prison critics call "tent city," they forgot that immigration prisoners can hire lawyers, and some of them even manage to do so. As a result, like the few other attorneys who represented clients there, my clients and I usually met inside an empty courtroom tucked into Willacy's administrative building. When the courtrooms were all being used, we just stood in the hallway between the courtrooms and the holding cells. Done meeting with me, my client walked back into the holding cell to join another ten or fifteen prisoners. Some were waiting for court; others were waiting for their lawyers. Ready to head back to the office, I looked around for the guard to let me out. There was no guard. I didn't know how long it had been since the guard had left, and I didn't know where he had gone, but it didn't matter. By this point it was me and a bunch of bored migrants in the back corridor of an immigration prison's courtrooms.

The prison system's rationale says this is a recipe for disaster. Reds and oranges—I very rarely met with blue-uniformed migrants—can't be unguarded. They are too volatile to be trusted.

And yet here we were: reds, oranges, blues, and me in my dark suit and with a pile of papers, standing and sitting around waiting for something to happen. For a guard to call a name for an audience with an immigration judge or to head back to the living quarters. Or just waiting to get back into my car and drive to the office. Collectively, we waited.

Nothing happened. The boredom weighed heavier, but nothing happened. It's remarkable only because ICE's detention practice suggests something far more exciting—more violent, more dangerous—should have happened. ICE's detention system, Obama-era reform chief Dora Schriro wrote, is "based largely upon the principles of command and control."[42] Why? Because, to ICE, the prisoners are too dangerous to be left to command their own destinies or to control the far more banal details of daily living: when to eat, who to visit, what to read or watch on television. Minnesota's Nobles County Jail, for example, let guards throw migrants into solitary confinement for "watching [the] Spanish channel on the TV."[43]

During that period of time in which I was stuck alongside a pool of locked-up migrants, the prisoners were effectively in charge, and nothing happened. Yet everything happened, because in boredom's triumph the entire scene illustrated the farce of ICE's command-and-control philosophy. Anytime a group of strangers gathers, there is the slim possibility of violence. Anytime a group of strangers is forcibly confined and subjected to systematic infantilization, the slim possibility grows. Despite this, the most palpable violence that day was the loud clang of the prison door when the guard later returned, and I was finally allowed to walk into the lobby, out the front door, and toward my car. No one acknowledged that the non-event illustrated the myth on which the prison regime's heavy-handedness is based.

6

THE MONEY

Most days are quiet in Milan, New Mexico. The Wow Diner offers a 1950s throwback experience with red booths lining the U-shaped building, and Kiva Café smothers its sopapillas in a red chili that screams New Mexico cuisine. If Milan's three thousand residents want more options, they can jump on Interstate 40 and head an hour and a half east to Albuquerque.

Unless they are locked up. Almost 40 percent of Milan's population lives inside the Cibola County Correctional Center, a monochromatic complex of beige buildings tucked behind the Wow Diner. Owned and run by CoreCivic, one of the two largest operators of private prisons in the United States, for many years the Cibola County Correctional Center held people convicted of entering the United States clandestinely, a federal crime. As convicted criminals, they were behind bars because they were being punished. Rings of concertina wire stretched across the tops of two layers of fencing leave a clear impression that punishment is the goal. In return for running the Milan prison, CoreCivic received a steady revenue stream from the Justice Department's Bureau of Prisons. Milan, meanwhile, came to value the prison's place in the town's slumbering economy. Roughly three hundred locals worked there.

When the Bureau of Prisons announced in July 2016 that it would not renew its contract with CoreCivic—at the time known as the Corrections Corporation of America (CCA)—effective

October 1 of that year, a shudder jolted the community. One resident, reflecting on the many prison employees she knew whose livelihoods were suddenly at risk, boiled down her thoughts to this: "It just . . . it sucks."[1]

For migrants' rights advocates, the Bureau of Prisons' announcement was welcome news they had long pushed for. The Milan prison had anything but a spotless history. A scathing investigative report published in *The Nation* earlier in 2016 chronicled the Cibola County Correctional Center's troubling practices. At various times throughout a sixteen-year period, inmates protested, guards tear-gassed, doctors were unavailable, and migrants died. Meanwhile, BOP regularly renewed the facility's contract.[2] Cibola, investigative reporter Seth Freed Wessler concluded, was "among the BOP's most problem-prone prisons."[3] This is saying something, particularly because BOP's private prison contractors were not known for their seamless operations. The fourteen private prisons under contract with BOP in 2016, the Justice Department's inspector general reported, were more likely to face safety and security problems than were prisons run by BOP's own staff.[4] A few months later, in the waning days of Obama's tenure, the Justice Department announced it would cut back its use of private prisons, a decision that the Trump administration reversed almost immediately upon taking power.

In the summer of 2016, the federal prison agency's decision to cut off the Cibola County facility seemed like its death knell. Who would want to do business with a prison so problematic that BOP had decided to sever its fifteen-year relationship? Seeing the imminent hit to employment rise ominously on the economic horizon, local officials and CCA executives sprung into action. The consequences of BOP's decision were frightening. For some officials, that made the path forward unambiguous. "My first option is for it to stay private because of the revenue the prison produces for the city of Milan," the local state senator, Democrat Clemente Sánchez, said.[5]

Before the month of October was out, Sánchez could breathe a sigh of relief, and CCA officials could celebrate success. Another contract was in place, this time with DHS. As the federal government's principal immigration-law enforcement arm, ICE is tasked with detaining people facing the possibility of forcible removal through the nation's immigration court system. Except for when ICE officers mistakenly pick up a U.S. citizen, everyone locked up on behalf of ICE is either a migrant waiting to learn whether she will be allowed to remain in the United States or a migrant already ordered removed awaiting the next available one-way spot on an airplane or bus. Unlike BOP, ICE doesn't imprison to punish. It imprisons to give the federal government time to decide who gets to be in the United States and who doesn't. This isn't punishment, courts tell us; it's just deciding where on the map people should stand.

A similar story played out in Willacy County in 2015. Tucked into an isolated part of deep South Texas, the Willacy County Processing Center held migrants facing possible removal through the immigration courts. And like with the Cibola County facility, it did so on behalf of ICE. When I represented migrants locked up in Willacy County, most of the people I saw were there because of some encounter with police officers—maybe a new conviction, sometimes an older conviction flagged upon returning to the United States from a trip abroad.

Willacy County was the picture of a minimum-security prison. The pungent odor of onions that fills the air when driving north along Highway 77 signals the industry that dominates the scenery and the local economy: agriculture. Up the road in the county seat of Raymondville, population 11,000, white farmers gather at the Whataburger fast-food joint for their morning coffee, while Latinos keep the abutting Stripes convenience store busy selling breakfast tacos and lunch plates. It isn't far from Stripes, where I often stopped, to the prison compound. Surrounded by farms, the Willacy County

Processing Center leaves an impression. Instead of brick and mortar, there are enormous tents enclosed by barbed wire.

The white canvas structures suggest a temporary holding facility. The truth is that the center was built in 2006. Private prison company Management and Training Corporation (MTC) held migrants there for days, months, or years—whatever it took for the immigration court case to unfold or the migrant to give up and agree to deportation. Migrants regularly complained about conditions inside. One former client, a man who had spent most of a decade in a federal prison for a serious drug-trafficking conviction and was later deported, told me that the prison was so poorly run that he would rather be back in a federal penitentiary. Advocates regularly criticized the poor medical care and frequency of sexual assaults. But little changed. ICE continued relying on MTC to house its detainees at the Willacy County facility.

Eventually, the complaints made their way to prominent journalist María Hinojosa, who took a television documentary crew inside Willacy County. In October 2011, Hinojosa and her team aired a harsh exposé of violence, mismanagement, and cover-ups on PBS stations nationwide. The documentary, *Lost in Detention*, bolstered the criticisms that detained migrants and their advocates had long voiced. Pushed into a corner, ICE finally severed its relationship with the Willacy County facility. It would no longer send people there while they waited to learn whether they would be allowed to remain in the United States.

Mirroring the Cibola County experience, one month later BOP stepped in to make use of the prison space suddenly freed. Because BOP is charged with confining people convicted of an offense, the facility got a name change. Instead of the Willacy County Processing Center, it became the Willacy County Correctional Center. Everything else remained untouched. The canvas tents stayed put. Barbed wire continued to divide the people inside from the rest of us outside. The same guards kept watch. The same private prison corporation, MTC, earned revenue from the federal government. People found themselves behind the barbed wire for the same reason: the federal government claimed they had violated immigration law. And the Willacy County coffers continued receiving payments for renting the jail to the federal government.

That is, until 2015, when inmates rebelled, leaving the facility uninhabitable. Three years later, it reopened with a different, but familiar, customer: ICE. As it geared up, the elected county judge complimented MTC in a company press release and celebrated its relaunch: "They are committed to the well-being of the people in their care. As you know, the last few years have been financially challenging for the county, so we look forward to this new facility and the economic benefits it will bring to our area."[6] The past, it seems, had been swept away.

More than a year after President Obama handed over the reins of government to President Trump, a top ICE official under Obama lamented the immigration prison system he'd overseen. John Sandweg, ICE's acting chief for a time, said that the size of the agency's detention population "weighed heavily on me." There were about five thousand people who deserved confinement, he estimated, because they posed a danger to the public. Everyone else should get an ankle bracelet or some other "safer, more humane" oversight built on high-tech surveillance. Instead, Sandweg had run one of the largest prison systems in the country. There was no way around it, he said, because "the public likes to hear 'detention.' It's billions of dollars for a talking point."[7]

Even accounting for the benefit of hindsight, Sandweg's words reek of a delusional attempt to make amends for his pivotal role in operating the nation's immigration prison regime. Under President Obama's watch, ICE agents locked up about 80 percent of the migrants they apprehended, even though most of the time agents had the legal authority to release them.[8] While ICE detained, the immigration prison system grew in size and importance. If we are to believe Sandweg, it did so despite the wishes of the people running it, but politics and money built immigration imprisonment in the 1980s and have made it impossible to shrink it. With every passing year, the immigration prison system's tentacles became more firmly embedded in immigration-law enforcement tactics.

These days, there is a host of elected officials, corporations, and individual investors who profit handsomely from immigration prisons. Their political and financial windfalls are hidden in plain sight. To the legislators who have expanded immigration imprisonment, this is a politically profitable policy choice. In the mid-1980s, the mayor of downcast Oakdale, Louisiana, successfully pitched his city to the INS, ICE's predecessor, as the site of one of the agency's first prisons. Mayor George Mowad saw immigration prisons as a "recession-proof" industry that could bring about Oakdale's "economic rebirth"—the worse the global economy got, the better it would get for Mowad's 7,200 constituents because bad job prospects elsewhere would bring migrants to the United States with or without the federal government's authorization.[9] To this day, Oakdale remains part of the federal government's immigration prison network.

Mayor Mowad's straightforward take on the value of an immigration prison was simple and self-serving, but not unique. Other elected officials have taken similar approaches. When a ship full of Chinese migrants became grounded near New York City in June 1993, a county commissioner in Perry County, Pennsylvania, said, "We tried like the dickens to get some of those Chinese. . . . The big reason we're doing all this is because we want to keep everybody working."[10] To these politicians, immigration prisons are just another type of economic development. If factories pull out or farming goes under, prisons promise quick returns. Soon after the ink dries on a contract, surveying and clearing, shoveling and pouring mark the beginnings of a massive construction or expansion project. Then come the guards, who need to be hired and trained. Later come the food vendors, maintenance staff, and, of course, health professionals like doctor-turned-mayor George Mowad. "It's going to be an economic boom," county judge David Davis of Haskell County, Texas, said of a prison that was reopening after a dispute between ICE and a private prison operator. "When you have the potential of having 150 or 160 employees that did not have a job six weeks ago and they come to work, you know the grocery stores, convenience stores, almost everyone is going to benefit from it." [11]

Prison towns aren't new to the United States. Generations of politicians have touted the financial benefits of locking up people, especially in rural communities. Immigration prisons are just adding a twist to this time-tested calculation. To politicians in city halls and state legislatures, the appeal of immigration prisons is simple. For the sake of confining migrants, the federal government is willing to send millions of dollars into small towns and big cities every day in the form of construction contracts, payroll taxes, and everything else that people with a steady paycheck tend to buy—from hamburgers to houses. If you're an elected official, your constituents get jobs. Better yet, someone else pays them.

An hour southeast of Phoenix, the town of Florence, Arizona, models the allure prisons have on rural communities. Some places are famous for making cars or boots. Florence builds prisons. Four years before Arizona became a state, prisoners were offloaded from a train and forced to start building their own cells in this out-of-the-way part of the Sonoran Desert. More than a century later, the state prison that they built still holds inmates, but it's far from alone. Florence now hosts eight prisons. ICE, the U.S. Marshals, and the Bureau of Prisons represent the federal government. "Florence was built around the prisons," write political scientists Roxanne Lynn Doty and Elizabeth Shannon Wheatley. [12] Combined, they hold roughly two-thirds of Florence's 25,000 residents. Public and private, state prisoners and county inmates. Everyone, it seems, can be locked up in Florence. During World War II, it held German prisoners of war and Japanese detainees removed from their West Coast homes. More famous are the murderers: from the "trunk murderess" Winnie Ruth Judd, who spent almost four decades locked up for two murders she said she didn't commit, to Robert Comer, a murderer and rapist who asked the courts to hurry up his death sentence.[13]

But the most profitable might be the migrants. Unlike county jails and state prisons, the cost of immigration prisons falls on the federal government. Whether it's the U.S. Marshals Service paying to detain people facing criminal prosecution for illegal entry or ICE paying to detain migrants awaiting a hearing before an immigration judge, the money comes from the same source: the United States Treasury. Cities, counties, and states pay almost nothing. To local elected officials, immigration prisons are a financial and political boon. Haskell County in Texas had just ponied up $22 million at the request of the Texas prison agency, when plans changed. "We were beginning construction and the State of Texas called and said we're not coming. . . . We now have ICE and it stays over 90 percent full," Judge Davis said.[14] Congress sends money to hire local workers, who in turn reward elected officials for their good fortune.

We can think of immigration prisons as a jobs program. For economically struggling regions where good-paying, steady jobs are hard to come by, immigration prisons are the twenty-first-century version of the Depression-era Works Progress Administration. Through the WPA, scores of workers laid the wires that lit up the Tennessee Valley, dressed up post offices with glorious murals, and recorded the memories of former slaves. Immigration prisons also provide jobs in out-of-the-way places. Only instead of hiring legions of unemployed workers to build important infrastructure and contribute to the nation's historical and artistic stock, the federal government now hires some people to build prisons and others to keep them running. And instead of bridges, timeless works of art, and priceless oral histories, we have the trauma of imprisonment to show for it. The consequences are different, but to mayors and city councilors, it is someone else's money for their gain.

With eye-catching dollar amounts moving from Washington to small towns, it is no surprise that elected officials fight to keep federally financed prisoners in their communities. "It's a money-making machine," the Houston chef turned immigration prisoner David Rodriguez told me. Whether in Cibola, Willacy, or somewhere else, when a facility verges on going out of business, local elected officials allied with company executives look for another customer for their job-providing prisons. Instead of trying to find other job prospects for their constituents, elected officials come to depend on the federal government's largesse and often show no interest in changing course. This is a form of what prison scholars Franklin Zimring and Gordon Hawkins referred to as the "correctional free lunch." [15] It's not that lunch is actually free; it's that someone else is picking up the bill. In Idaho, the Jerome County sheriff went after an ICE contract for months as a way of making easy money. When those negotiations stalled, the sheriff turned to the U.S. Marshals, which pays as much as ICE: $75 per day per person. And when local politicians urged the sheriff to take the state prison chief's money, the sheriff balked. "It's a matter of economics," the sheriff said, comparing the federal government's rate to the $45 per day he could expect from the state. "I think the people that voted for the jail in Jerome County expect us to make the best decision to get this bond paid off early," he said, referring to the county's prison debt. [16]

For all their costs, immigration prisons often fail to deliver the benefits they promise. As the sheriff of Jerome County, Idaho, learned, sometimes immigration prison contracts don't pan out.

Then there are promises that private prisons make. Private prison corporations tout guaranteed revenue like a magical elixir to cure unemployment. To entice the federal government to open its immigration-prison funding stream, they convince local officials to take on new debt for prison construction projects. Maybe build a new facility or simply fix up and expand an older one. Either way, taxpayers wind up with debt and a promise that the federal government will pay. With bipartisan support for immigration prisons stretching back to the late 1980s, this strategy frequently works out for a time. But just as the federal government can swoop in with its big purse, it can also pull out.

When that happens, local governments are left with piles of debt and empty prison beds, a reality that Cibola knows all too well. Officials there had become so thoroughly hooked on the federal government's money that they were spending it before receiving it. After the county bounced a check for $7 million— money it owed CoreCivic—officials admitted that the county had spent $9.5 million over three years that it didn't have.[17] Cibola is extreme, but it's not alone in facing the hard realities of the immigration-prison business. In Ramsey County, Minnesota, which includes state capital St. Paul, ICE's inmates were costing the sheriff $160 per day, but the federal government was only paying $80.[18] Over in Texas, McLennan County officials facing $49 million in jail debt hired a private prison corporation, LaSalle Corrections, "because of LaSalle's reputation for bringing federal inmates to their facilities," and offered ICE three hundred beds.[19]

Once the jobs come, elected officials turn their attention to keeping them in town. In Georgia's Irwin County, the chairman of the Board of Commissioners lamented the possibility that the local immigration prison would shutter: "If it closes, then everybody loses their jobs . . . and the inmates go back to wherever they came from, but we hope that it never gets to that."[20] Winning a contract only to lose it later hurts just as much, maybe more. Just

like in Cibola County, when the Willacy County facility lost its
contract with BOP to house convicted immigration offenders (after previously losing its contract with ICE to house people facing
the possibility of removal from the United States), local officials
worried about layoffs for the prison staff. "I feel for the staff," one
official said. "It must be very stressful to be sitting in limbo."[21]
The former mayor was more direct: "We need everybody to be employed. We need those prisoners."[22]

Pinal County, Arizona, where Florence serves as the county
seat, has fewer college graduates than the rest of the state and
more people without jobs. CoreCivic's footprint in the county's
economy is big. In Florence, the company runs two immigration
prisons. It has four more in Eloy, twenty-five miles farther southwest in Pinal County. The Central Arizona Detention Center
Complex-East and its counterpart, the Central Arizona Detention Center Complex-West, in Florence are all-in-one facilities.
They both hold inmates for ICE, the U.S. Marshals, and the Bureau of Prisons. Twelve-foot-high fences surround concrete cor-
ridors and steel doors. With room for more than four thousand
prisoners, CoreCivic can house 15 percent of the town's population. Back in 2015, the company—then called CCA—was charging ICE $87.26 per inmate per day.[23] At this rate, the company
could easily bring in hundreds of thousands of dollars every day
from its Florence operations alone.

CoreCivic isn't the only immigration prison operation in town.
ICE runs its own facility, the Florence Service Processing Center.
The "Service" in the name harkens back to its time as an INS facility, but it's actually much older than that. It got its start housing World War II prisoners of war, then had a second life under
BOP control. The INS was its third operator, and ICE its fourth.
Even though it owns the FSPC, ICE gets operational help from
outside vendors. In 2009 it awarded a little-known company, As-
set Protection and Security Services LP, a $184 million contract

to run the cafeteria, provide ground transportation, and keep the facility secure for twelve months.[24] A few years later, in 2017, ICE reported to Congress that it spent $222.05 to house each of its 371 Florence detainees every night.[25]

Costs would almost certainly be higher if ICE couldn't pay detainees $1.00 per day to staff the kitchen. In the cold language of bureaucratic standards, ICE says, "Detainees shall receive monetary compensation for work. . . . The compensation is at least $1.00 (USD) per day."[26] The government says this is a "stipend" for participating in the "Detainee Voluntary Work Program."[27] Alejandro Menocal calls it "forced labor." For three months, he was an inmate worker at a private prison outside Denver run by GEO Group, CoreCivic's main competitor. Now he's the lead plaintiff in the first-of-its-kind lawsuit claiming the company demands cheap labor or inmates risk solitary confinement.[28] Another former ICE prisoner, Robinson Martinez, would likely agree with him. Back in 2013, he complained that an officer for the private prison woke him at 3:00 a.m. and instructed him to start cleaning the facility. "I said 'I do not have to work because this is a volunteer work," he wrote in a complaint letter to ICE. "She responded by saying 'well then I will right [sic] you up.'" Too many write-ups, and he could end up in segregation, Martinez feared.[29]

Despite these problems, to the variety of third-party actors invested in immigration imprisonment, it is financially profitable. Private prison corporations publicly claim to be agnostic about laws expanding imprisonment, but this is a tough claim to swallow given how much they reap from immigration prisons. Roughly two-thirds of ICE's detainees are held in private facilities.[30] With an average daily population of 38,106 in fiscal year 2017, that is 24,768 people in private facilities. At an average cost of $128.88 per day for each person, the private prison industry as a whole gets $3.2 million from ICE alone every single day.[31]

Thinking about the private prison–government relationship in a different way, one-quarter of CoreCivic's revenue comes from ICE.[32] The same is true of 19 percent of GEO Group's business.[33] Add contracts with the USMS and BOP to the mix and it becomes clear just how dependent the leading private prison corporations are on federal revenue. Roughly half of GEO Group and CoreCivic's money originates with the federal government.[34]

Prison companies are more than happy to remind politicians about their role in boosting the local economy. In February 2010, Arizona was set to jump onto the international stage as it considered passing what was at the time the harshest piece of immigration legislation in many years. As legislators debated and ordinary people took to the streets—in favor and in strident opposition— CCA (as CoreCivic was then known) issued an economic analysis touting its contributions to the state's economy. "The study's findings are compelling," the study's company-hired authors claimed. Statewide, CCA had 2,773 employees and indirectly supported another 1,700 jobs. That spells $435 million of economic activity and $26.2 million in tax revenue. In Pinal County, home to CCA's six prisons in Florence and Eloy, the company's presence, the report went on in bold type, is "already paying off." With a payroll that includes nearly 5 percent of the county's workers, it's the biggest non-government employer.[35] When the study was publicly issued, the company ran a press release claiming it "proves public-private partnerships in corrections energize[] state economies," and the *Prescott News* repeated many of the study's claims.[36] Numbers like these are nothing a politician can ignore. Even if someone wanted to stand up to CCA—and few in towns like Florence appear interested—they would need a ready answer to the obvious challenge of finding an economic substitute that is as easy to imagine as the brick-and-mortar prisons down the street.

Private prison corporations do their part to limit second-guessing by regularly contributing to candidates and elected officials. From 2017 to 2018, the three largest private prison corporations operating in the United States—GEO Group, CoreCivic, and Utah-based Management & Training Corporation—sent over $800,000 to candidates' campaigns. Collectively, the private prison industry spent over three times that amount in lobbying: $3.5 million in 2017 alone. While most of their financial largess went to Republicans, Henry Cuellar, a Democratic member of Congress representing parts of the Texas border, was the fourth-highest recipient.[37] In 2014, Cuellar partnered with his fellow Texan, Republican senator John Cornyn, to sponsor a bill that would have expanded detention of children—what the proposal called "mandatory protective custody"—while government officials considered their asylum applications.[38] The bill failed, but it did win Cuellar a "Humpday Hall of Shame" award from the activist group Grassroots Leadership.[39]

What happens in Washington certainly matters, but private prisons don't ignore the role states play. National Public Radio, for example, credited private prisons with a "quiet, behind-the-scenes effort to help draft and pass Arizona Senate Bill 1070."[40] By 2017, some of the industry's allies had lost any pretense of keeping their relationship behind the scenes. A Republican state legislator in Texas pushing a bill that would have made it much easier for private prisons to detain children there was explicit about who wrote the proposal. "I've known the lady who's their lobbyist for a long time," Representative John Raney said to reporters. "That's where the legislation came from."[41] The following year, GEO gave him $1,500, tripling the total amount the company had given Raney in his seven-year political career.[42]

Despite their substantial coffers, private prison corporations can't operate without additional financial backing. As publicly-traded companies, CoreCivic and GEO frequently submit reports to the Securities and Exchange Commission. Looking at those documents closely reveals how entangled private prisons are with run-of-the-mill financial institutions. Accounting giant Ernst & Young audits CoreCivic's financial controls, while its competitor Grant Thornton audits GEO Group.[43] For many years, major banking institutions like Bank of America and Wells Fargo helped the companies obtain credit.[44] Both private prison companies depend on constant credit to do everything from making large purchases of land and facilities to paying for operations. When 2017 ended, for example, CoreCivic had $694 million available in an existing credit line and $1.4 billion in debt.[45] By mid-2019, their ability to get more loans was cast into doubt when major banks began falling in line with anti–private prison activists. In January, Wells Fargo announced it was no longer seeking business from private prison corporations. In March, JPMorgan Chase said that it would no longer bankroll private prisons. Still, halfway into the year both major prison corporations were doing well. CoreCivic reported $490 million in total revenue and GEO Group another $614 million—all in a single quarter.

"Who owns these companies?" a student in one of my classes asked me not too long ago. "I do, I assume," I said. Like most other salaried university employees, I participate in a retirement account run by industry giant TIAA. Most of my retirement savings consists of mutual fund purchases. Maybe it's careless, but all I do is pick an estimated retirement year, and TIAA does the rest. They invest contributions that I make and those that my employer makes on my behalf in a mix of financial instruments that I don't begin to understand. But after that conversation with my students, I tried figuring out whether my assumption was correct. Do I actually support the private prison industry that profits from warehousing migrants? I failed. I couldn't find a list of specific investments.

The truth is that private prisons are owned by a diverse range of private and public investors. In March 2019, pension funds for Ohio public employees and New York teachers each held over 250,000 shares of CoreCivic. With eighteen million shares, Vanguard Group, a suburban Philadelphia company that offers mutual funds and 401(k) plans, among other investments, was CoreCivic's largest owner.[46] Vanguard held a similarly large number of GEO's shares, putting it at the top of that company's ownership list as well.[47] Retirement accounts for public employees in California, New York, Alabama, and several more states held shares of GEO Group. On both companies' investor lists is my retirement account manager, TIAA. With just over 234,000 shares of CoreCivic priced at $24.00 and about 460,000 shares of GEO priced at roughly $23 each, educators like me have a $5.6 million stake in CoreCivic and $10.6 million thrown in with GEO. For now, at least, my wealth depends in part on GEO's success locking up migrants.

My complicity in private prisons highlights the difficulty of scaling back immigration imprisonment. Cutting off CoreCivic and GEO's tentacles means cutting off part of my retirement financial cushion. I can't count on public pensions to live a comfortable life in old age. If I don't save part of my income and invest it wisely, the likelihood that I will end my days in poverty jumps. Growing up in public housing, I remember poverty well and have no interest revisiting that part of my childhood. Perversely, it means that I am buying my future comfort at the expense of other people's present discomfort—and far worse.

This doesn't sit well with me, but figuring out what to do about it is daunting. Until my student's question, I hadn't seriously thought about the possibility of shifting my own money out of the private prison industry. Wouldn't that amount to a one-person boycott? I spend a good deal of time talking with activists and reading their emails, but I couldn't recall having been asked to do this. On the contrary, I can't count the number of fundraising pitches I receive. Like most people, my willingness to give away money is tied to my financial health. The larger my bank account is, the larger and more frequently that I donate to causes I support—including the very organizations whose mission it is to help migrants.

So, I started searching for advice. The Prison Divestment Campaign, a coalition of activists and unions, says it "is working to divest from criminalization and incarceration, and demand reparations and reinvestment in our communities," but it focuses on public investors like cities and large institutional investors like universities. It asks nothing of individual investors like me.

To make sense of this, I spoke with Daniel Carillo, a long-time divestment advocate. Activists chose to focus on institutional investors, Carillo told me, as a strategic matter. Limited resources mean that they couldn't prioritize individual investors, because that's not where the big pots of money are. That makes sense. No matter how well my investment portfolio does, it will never compare to my employer's. Still, Carillo wasn't willing to give me a clean out. People like me, he said, should move money into socially responsible investment funds that screen out the prison industry. As I learned while scouring my own investments, private prison corporations that are publicly traded—companies like CoreCivic and GEO—are easiest to spot.

When my money is tied up with my employer, as is true for many professional employees, the road to divestment begins with education. Track down a contact person at the investment fund and ask for a pension portfolio. Raise tough questions. And think hard about organizing co-workers to demand prison-free investments. The socially responsible investment industry will respond, Carillo said. "Their bottom line is money," he explained. "When we first spoke to them, they did not think the prison industry was a great thing to add. Now they see that this is a growing business, so it's a money-maker." The response to exploitative capitalism might start with something as simple as identifying alternative paths to wealth creation.

Part III

TOWARD A DIFFERENT TOMORROW

7

ABOLISHING IMMIGRATION PRISONS

Standing where we are now, with more people locked up than ever before for daring to move across the face of the Earth, it is hard to imagine policing immigration law without prisons. Since the days of President Jimmy Carter's administration, immigration prisons have enjoyed bipartisan support.

With President Trump's election, the rhetoric and reality of immigration imprisonment has become more corrosive than ever. From the start, his election promised more imprisonment. His first attorney general, Jeff Sessions, worked hard to bring that promise to life. His second, William Barr, picked up where Sessions left off, and there is certainly nothing on the political horizon suggesting that immigration prisons are losing favor in Washington or anywhere else. In the summer of 2018, President Trump's immigration enforcement practices careened into what, for many people, was the previously unthinkable image of government officials stripping children from their parents. I saw children no older than six jumping rope under a beating Arizona sun, their bodies so light that the rope picked up more dirt than their feet did from the parched floor. Tall fences, electronic locks, and a twenty-four-hour surveillance team make sure that few children think hard about leaving.

Sharon Phillips, a New York City lawyer who has repeatedly visited the country's largest family-only facility in Texas, adds much-needed context. "This isn't about Trump. It didn't start with him," she told me. Indeed, under President Obama, the federal government first closed Bush-era family immigration prisons. A few years later, the Obama administration opened new family immigration prisons. Trump didn't start family imprisonment, but, as Phillips points out, "Trump escalated it."

If Donald Trump's rapid rise from tabloid fame to foul-mouthed president teaches anything, it's that politics change, time moves forward, and what was previously unimaginable can one day become the new normal. In the Biblical story of Joshua's attack on the walled city of Jericho, it took patience and strategy, but finally "the wall fell down flat, so that the people went up into the city." [1] With the right mix of inspiration and organization, prison walls can come tumbling down.

For years, lawyers and organizers have tried to fix immigration prisons. Often, they have had some success. When lawyers and family members complained that people were getting lost inside ICE's facilities, the agency created a website to track the people in its custody. When advocates complained that sexual assaults were rampant in ICE's network, Congress extended the Prison Rape Elimination Act. Even President Trump has scaled back some of his administration's worst excesses. Public outcry over family separations convinced him to bar Border Patrol officers from sending parents for criminal prosecution and children to child-only facilities under the pretense of needing to talk in another jail cell.

And yet it remains extremely difficult for lawyers and relatives to keep in touch with detainees, because ICE moves them around the country without regard for whether an hours-long flight is a realistic option for advocates and family members. Rapes are banned, but survivors of sexual violence still find legal roadblocks on the path to justice. In one case, a federal court dismissed a lawsuit filed by eight women who were raped by an immigration prison guard. The guard had admitted his guilt in a separate criminal prosecution, and ICE had violated an internal policy by letting the guard escort the women alone, but that wasn't enough for the court. In the view of the conservative Fifth Circuit Court of Appeals, violating a policy intended to avoid sexual assault isn't the same as showing that a "substantial risk of serious harm exists."[2]

Seeing only the harsh edge of an immigration policy that has grown even harsher under President Trump can turn even the most reasonable observer into a cynic. I prefer to search for hope, to think of the Trump moment as an opportunity to revisit assumptions. And no assumption is harder to uproot than the hold that immigration prisons have on people who make immigration policy and those who contest it. Without escaping the immigration prison's walls, it might be impossible to escape the prison system's racism and mass commodification of human life.

Freedom for thousands of people considered too dangerous or untrustworthy to live outside walls won't happen overnight. In a series of essays, Angela Davis put forward a helpful way of thinking about a world with more freedom and fewer prisons. Abolition, she says, isn't just about toppling what already exists. It has to be about building up something else too. Abolition "involves reimagining institutions, ideas, and strategies, and creating new institutions, ideas, and strategies that will render prisons obsolete," she argues.[3] Without a constructive component, the destructive part of abolition will leave a gaping hole in the policy landscape. And that hole, we can expect, will prove fertile ground for other forms of exploitation to grow.

No better example exists about the risks of destructive abolition than slavery's aftermath. Even now, the centuries-old practice of turning humans into commodities stands apart from other instances of cruelty. In his infamous opinion in *Dred Scott v. Sandford*, the pre–Civil War case in which the Supreme Court concluded that a black man could not claim U.S. citizenship, Justice Roger Taney captured slavery's ethos: "[the black man] had no rights which the white man was bound to respect."[4] In the eyes of the law, black people were things to be bought, sold, and gifted, raped and beaten, worked to exhaustion or death, criminalized and killed. Black men were valued for their ability to create wealth. Black women were prized for their ability to make new things and, through childbirth, new slaves. The law enabled social and racial control.

When that horrible institution collapsed in the flames of the war-torn nation, there was reason for hope. Abolitionists had long pushed for slavery's demise to be paired with meaningful reparations. They wanted to destroy the social institution and upend the legal regime at the same time that slavery's winners made amends—real, concrete wealth transfers—to their newly freed neighbors. For a moment, dreams seemed like they might become reality.

And then hope gave way to the brutality of raw power. Sharecropping reconfigured economic relations, but not the racial order. Criminal prosecution gave legal cover to old habits: controlling blacks' movements through laws against loitering, for example, and exploiting their physical labor. Violence remained a favorite terror tactic.

Early in the twentieth century, W.E.B. DuBois pilloried the course that abolition had taken. In his monumental *The Souls of Black Folk*, DuBois wrote, "What did such a mockery of freedom mean? Not a cent of money, not an inch of land, not a mouthful of victuals,—not even ownership of the rags on his back. Free!"[5] To DuBois, abolishing slavery required more than ending the legally permissible ownership of human beings. To him, it meant rectifying the sin of profiting from centuries of exploitation. It meant redistributing wealth from the people who had taken it through the violent tip of a cracking whip and giving it to the people whose hands had actually tilled the soil. For abolition to become meaningful, legal change couldn't stand alone. Severing the literal chains wasn't enough. It needed to be accompanied by changes to a culture built around white people's exploitation of black people. Simply, DuBois believed that a social transformation was necessary. For that to happen, white supremacy itself had to be uprooted. To his dismay, exploitation in the form of slavery ended, but exploitation did not. It just took a different form.

Reforming immigration prisons carries a similar Achilles' heel. They are built, they expand, they evolve, they know no failure. Angela Davis lobbed a similar critique at prison reform, claiming "more frequently than not, these reforms have ultimately solidified the institution."[6] In his history of prisons, *Discipline and Punish*, French philosopher Michel Foucault wrote, "Prison 'reform' is virtually contemporary with the prison itself: it constitutes, as it were, its programme."[7] From this perspective, efforts to reform prisons entrench them further rather than threaten their existence. Making immigration prisons nicer may drive migrants' confinement further into the United States' legal system, but more worryingly, trying to fix the worst parts of immigration prisons risks turning the prisons that remain into symbols of enlightened policymaking. To a United Nations human-rights official, a converted nursing home in Pennsylvania represents "best practices" in immigration detention.[8] To Diego Rivera Osorio, it's where he learned to walk.

Left to the slow churn of reform, prisons can morph into a warped humanitarianism. The very word *penitentiary* derives from the Latin word for repentance, *paenitentia*. Like the early U.S. prisons, the theory underlying imprisonment imagines a space in which moral deviants repent. By seeking forgiveness, they can overcome the moral stain of their transgressions and experience new life as morally upstanding members of the community. Following this me-and-my-God model, Philadelphia's Eastern State Penitentiary, for instance, was designed to allow for maximum communion with God. Inmates were kept in one-person cells from which they could see no one except the guard. They could communicate with no one except their jailer, their God, and their conscience. To the moral reformers who backed this experiment in punitive social redemption in the Quaker-influenced city, the new penitentiary was a lost soul's moral sanctuary. With the body caged, the soul could be cradled.

But thought of another way, Eastern State was an experience in punitive double-sidedness. Corporal punishment ensured that inmates had no control over their bodies. The crushing power of isolation ensured that they didn't have much more control over their minds. Traveling across the United States in 1842, Charles Dickens stopped in Philadelphia, where he marveled at the city's hospital and waterworks—"no less ornamental than useful," he concluded. Its new prison, however, dismayed Dickens. "I hold this slow and daily tampering with the mysteries of the brain, to be immeasurably worse than any torture of the body," he wrote. With singing prose, he went on to explain the horror of being complicit in such cruelty. "I solemnly declare, that with no rewards or honours could I walk a happy man . . . with the consciousness that one human creature, for any length of time, no matter what, lay suffering this unknown punishment in his silent cell." [9]

Immigration prisons have followed a similar confinement-as-humanitarianism pattern. When Chinese migrants were detained in the dockside warehouses, good-hearted advocates criticized conditions inside, leading the federal government to build its own facilities on San Francisco Bay's Angel Island, turning misery from temporary cruelty to bricks-and-mortar permanency.

A similar story repeated itself a century later with the Krome Avenue Detention Center. In 1980, the Carter administration turned an old missile site near Miami into a makeshift detention center for Cubans and Haitians. Living conditions were bad all around, but for the southern portion of the camp, where Haitians were housed, things were outright deplorable. A lawyer for detained Haitians said conditions were "atrocious." "We do not

consider those sites fit for human habitation," a spokesperson for
the Florida Department of Health added. "It is an intolerable situation." Soon federal officials invested in upgrades, transforming
this bit of South Florida swamp "into a more permanent facility
designed to discipline and to hold unwanted refugees," writes historian Jana K. Lipman.[10]

Writing about legal challenges to immigration detention practices in the United States in the 1980s, historian Carl Lindskoog
describes this trend. After the Carter administration suddenly
began its hastily implemented, ad-hoc detention of Haitians, the
detainees sued, claiming the government had failed to follow required procedures for shifting its policy. The INS responded by
adopting a formal detention policy.[11] When advocates complained
to the Reagan administration that the federal prison system was
over capacity largely because of too many Haitian and Cuban migrants, administration officials asked Congress for more money,
and the INS responded by spreading its detainees across nine hundred state and local jails.[12] "Each challenge led to the development
of a more resilient legal, political, and economic rationale for its
existence," notes Lindskoog.[13]

A similar pattern has repeated itself more recently. When
George W. Bush occupied the White House, ICE started splitting
parents who were caught alongside their children. To Congress,
it was outrageous that ICE would tread on the sanctity of family
life. In response, the immigration agency recommissioned a former medium-security prison as a stand-alone family prison called
the Hutto Family Residential Center. In the dry wit of the world's
leading researcher on immigration prisons, Michael Flynn, "detaining families at Hutto was apparently meant to protect an important right—the right to family life."[14]

Recently, we have seen more of the same. During the summer
of 2014, the Obama administration threw open a family prison
in Artesia, New Mexico. One of the first attorneys to arrive there,

Julia Braker, recalls surprise at the number of sick migrants and blames living conditions. "It seemed pretty intentionally created by the government," she told me. She had the impression that "it was supposed to be miserable." Later that year, the federal government partnered with a private prison corporation to open a permanent facility in rural Texas. The South Texas Family Residential Center in Dilley, about an hour south of San Antonio, is the largest families-only facility in the government's immigration prison arsenal.

Fast-forward to 2018, and the pattern repeats itself. In a mean-spirited spat, the Trump administration began taking children from their parents, prosecuting the adults criminally, and sending kids to government-financed, privately run "shelters" from which they can't leave. Government officials struggled to say how many families they separated. Meanwhile, the Trump administration official in charge of overseeing the child-only prisons fought all the way to the Supreme Court to block girls from accessing abortion services. When news broke of children being taken from their parents—sometimes literally while the kids were asleep in a mother's arms, at other times through outright lies—criticism came from every corner. Even Melania Trump voiced her opposition. Eventually, the president ended that practice, only to replace it with an effort to detain more families together.

Government officials aren't beyond blaming advocates for prison expansion. Reagan's attorney general, William French Smith, claimed Haitians were confined longer than other migrants because they insisted on speaking to lawyers and filing asylum applications.[15] Most shocking, at one point in the mid-1990s, advocates for Haitian migrants even lobbied the Clinton administration to reopen a detention center at Guantánamo, Cuba, because that was better than the government's proposal of reviewing asylum claims in Haiti or on board a navy ship.[16]

Clearly, prisons have become part of the psyche of immigration law. Decades into its modern growth spurt, immigration prisons have grown roots that keep the industry thriving. End one contract, and another one will take its place. This is what happened in Milan, New Mexico, when BOP cut off a prison, only for it to be saved by ICE. It's what happened in Willacy County, Texas, when ICE pulled out and BOP stepped in. Then BOP pulled out and ICE returned.

Without cutting off immigration prisons at their root, they will continue to resurrect themselves. So long as the federal government is committed to a security-first philosophy that imagines migrants as dangerous outsiders—aliens—who pose an existential threat to the nation itself, then it makes all the sense in the world that it will turn to the power of confinement.

Legislators, lawyers, and even many activists have bought into the need for prisons such that it is almost impossible for anyone to think outside the box. Books are constantly written about the problems with imprisonment and lawsuits filed challenging prisons' worst excesses, but in the context of immigration, few people have asked the all-important question: "Are prisons obsolete?" as Angela Davis put it in 2003. Thinking about it another way, would immigration law crumble if prisons ceased to exist?

We certainly don't need prisons to enforce immigration laws. During the early 1980s, when immigration imprisonment was ramping up, opposition came from all quarters. The Democratic governor of Florida led a state lawsuit against the INS over conditions inside a Miami facility. Far to the north, Republican congressman David Martin helped derail plans to confine migrants at an army base in his district near the Canadian border. The federal government itself questioned whether the INS was up to the task of confinement, concluding that an INS center "is not an efficient long-term custody solution." [17]

In his history of early prison profiteers, Malcolm Feeley writes that it "was not always a foregone conclusion" that prisons would be used to punish people for their transgressions.[18] For centuries before the United States split away from the United Kingdom, English courts worked with private shipping companies to remove serious offenders, literally, by forcibly transporting them across the Atlantic. To the Crown, this was a great deal. It punished offenders, showed a strong willingness to fight crime, and cost very little money: people could request transportation in lieu of death, and they could pay for it themselves or indenture themselves to a private shipping company. Most people are aware that a version of this happened in Australia, but it thrived along the eastern seaboard of North America longer and earlier. Transportation to North America came to a rapid halt with the colonial uprising that eventually led to U.S. independence. Almost at once, "entrepreneurs," as Feeley calls them, pitched prisons as a cheap, effective way of removing offenders from society.

And so punishment through mobility, through moving offenders elsewhere, became punishment through immobility, through putting them behind bars. Like in the days before U.S. independence, migrants experienced legal disapproval by being forcibly relocated. And like with the beginnings of criminal imprisonment, migrants eventually began to suffer that same disapproval through forced confinement.

I don't pretend to have a step-by-step plan for getting from a policy that imprisons half a million migrants annually to one that ensnares zero. The radical activist group Mijente is among the few organizations calling for the abolition "of all forms of immigration detention," but even they don't pretend to know how to navigate the politics of migration to reach that goal.[19] No one does, because no one can. If it took seven days for the Old Testament Jews to fell the walls of Jericho, surely it will take much longer for mere mortals to tumble the walls of immigration prisons.

Reforms that merely reorganize and reproduce coercion won't

get us any nearer to a world without immigration prisons. It's not enough to shift the bounds of who should be locked up. The United States has tried that. When Congress declared that anyone convicted of an aggravated felony must be detained, they identified three serious crimes that fall into this category. Now there are twenty-one types of aggravated felonies.

Nor is it acceptable to support reforms that simply inject some twists into the path toward confinement. ICE's existing alternatives to detention programs fall into this camp. Though they have taken different forms over the years, these initiatives always involve intrusive surveillance. Typically, they also come with around-the-clock GPS monitoring through clunky ankle bracelets that reek of punishment. Fail to meet the monitoring requirements and a migrant loses any chance at freedom. Worse, ICE uses these programs as alternative ways of keeping tabs on people who don't need to be watched—people who are grounded in the United States and are therefore unlikely to miss court dates, and people who show no inkling of violence. These aren't people who would be detained and are now being allowed a semblance of liberty. Instead, these are people who should never have been detained in the first place. Treating ICE's alternatives to detention as a step up is only possible after accepting the agency's premise that everyone deserves confinement.

But some reforms can better approach an abolitionist future. Reforms that reduce the immigration-law enforcement system's reach into migrants' lives might help end immigration imprisonment. For example, the United States should disentangle ICE's power to detain from the criminal justice system. A racially biased, deeply flawed criminal justice system that skews against poor people shouldn't be the foundation on which civil detention rests. It wasn't defensible at the turn of the twentieth century, when dockside warehouses in San Francisco were dubbed "Chinese jails," and it's not acceptable now. At the same time, Congress should throw

the federal crimes of illegal entry and illegal reentry into the dust-
bin of legislative history. What benefit has the United States received since the Bush administration prioritized these sections of
the federal penal code?

If those seem far-fetched, then we can start by giving every migrant a lawyer, whether they can pay for it or not, then add other
support like social workers, while handing everyone a work permit so they can sustain themselves while they raise their legal
claims. The country's first initiative to provide lawyers for everyone held in a particular immigration prison facing deportation,
the New York Immigrant Family Unity Project, led to a surge in
the number of people who were released. Once out of prison, almost everyone showed up for court dates. During its first three
years, 10 of 611 Family Unity Project clients released from prison
failed to show up to court without the judge's permission. That's
a 98 percent success rate. Legal representation also increased the
odds that migrants would win their court cases. Before getting a
lawyer through the program, 4 percent of migrants successfully
fended off removal. With the help of a lawyer, the number jumped
to 42 percent.[20]

None of this is a surprise. Immigration prisoners aren't the
wandering souls that politicians like to make them out to be.
Many have deep ties to the United States. One out of three people
held by ICE in the summer of 2018 had been in the United States
for at least one year. Almost 20 percent had been here for at least
ten years. People with the most serious type of criminal records—
who, by law, must be locked up while waiting for the immigration
courts to process their cases—tend to have spent a long time in the
United States. According to one study, on average fifteen years.[21]

In addition, when a legal process gives people a meaningful opportunity to participate and takes their concerns seriously, they
comply. Known in the academic literature as "procedural justice,"
the idea boils down to simple fairness. People can sniff out a sham

legal process. If the rules are stacked against someone, the outcome seems rigged. But if everyone seems to be getting a fair deal, then people will go with it, even if they don't like the outcome. Nuremberg prosecutor and Supreme Court Justice Robert Jackson captured this concept at its most basic. "Severe substantive laws can be endured if they are fairly and impartially applied," he wrote in a 1953 dissenting opinion.[22]

Emily Ryo, the legal scholar, is one of the few people to seriously study this phenomenon in the immigration prison context. Analyzing surveys of almost six hundred ICE detainees, Ryo found "a significant relationship between immigrant detainees' fair treatment perceptions and their perceived obligation to obey U.S. immigration authorities." Interestingly, this group of migrants was more committed to following the law than what studies of people living freely in the United States typically find.[23] What this means for immigration prisons is straightforward, even if it does fly in the face of decades of bipartisan political rhetoric. If we want migrants to show up for court dates, treat them fairly. It's really that simple. Prisons aren't just unnecessary; they're counterproductive.

The government's own experience proves this. Almost since it returned to immigration imprisonment, it has been experimenting with alternatives to confinement. While President Reagan was still in office, the INS worked with the migration arm of the United States Catholic Conference to move into the community some of its most notorious detainees, the Mariel Cubans made famous by Al Pacino's *Scarface*. For a dozen years from 1987 to 1999, the Catholic group provided education, job training, substance abuse treatment, and weekly meetings to fifty to sixty Cubans annually. Three-quarters had no problems meeting the program's requirements.[24] Overlapping with the Cuban initiative, in 1997 the INS partnered with the Vera Institute of Justice to run an intensive compliance-support pilot program in the New York and New

Jersey area. Instead of confining migrants, the INS sent migrants selected for the initiative to live with community sponsors. Once outside, migrants were educated about the immigration court process and the importance of complying with court orders, kept up-to-date on court dates, and referred to legal counsel.[25] Eighty-five percent of participants in the Clinton-era program kept showing up to court.[26]

These aren't the only success stories. In the late 1990s, the INS had on its hands people who had already been ordered deported because of criminal records, but for whom the government couldn't get necessary travel documents. It planned to deal with them by locking them up for however long it took—indefinitely, if necessary. Catholic Charities stepped in. From 1999 to 2000, it moved those people out of prison. By the time he was tapped to participate, one man had been in INS prisons for seven years. Once enrolled, everyone got a place to live, information about program expectations, and help with jobs. Of the first twenty-one people to participate, twenty had no problems.[27]

Success stories like these aren't ancient history. They aren't even the most recent examples. During the Obama years, ICE partnered with Lutheran Immigration and Refugee Services to provide ten migrant families with full-service case management. The faith-based organization's staff helped the families find housing, educated migrants about the legal process, and provided legal assistance. The program was tiny. It was funded primarily by two private foundations and was intended to show that robust case management could compete with detention. The results were remarkable, but not surprising. One hundred percent of families did what immigration officials told them.[28]

What makes these programs worth talking about isn't just that they work, but that they work without intrusive law enforcement–style oversight. Unlike prison life, none required days behind steel doors and concertina wire. None involved handing over cash to pay for release on bond. Contrast that to standard practice in immigration courts, where judges hand out bonds averaging as much as $80,500.[29] Most of the time, no one had an electronic bracelet strapped to their ankle, but contrast that with ICE's willingness to use electronic bracelets on people with no criminal records and with deep ties to the community. And none of these initiatives relied simplistically on criminal records to bar participation, a stark contrast to federal judges who deny bond to immigration-crime defendants more often than they do to people charged with any other federal crime. Instead of superficial assumptions about dangerous migrants who are all too willing to disappear into the anonymous masses of migrant America, each initiative used a straightforward cocktail of support to increase compliance: individualized education and legal representation combined with community collaboration. These programs prove that it is possible to comply with immigration requirements and enjoy the freedom most of us take for granted.

For thirty years, the federal government has had at its disposal meaningful options to ensure that migrants show up to court and don't endanger the community. Without enlarging the number of people incarcerated or expanding the government's surveillance of people it wouldn't otherwise keep tabs on, these projects cost pennies to the dollar compared to detention. But instead of pouring money and ingenuity into them, it has always chosen to kill these projects, instead prioritizing detention and alternatives to detention that involve similarly heavy surveillance. Over and over again, imprisonment has beat out freedom.

That we don't already take these basic steps toward injecting fairness into immigration proceedings and instead rely on the easy claim that migrants are too unscrupulous to merit liberty reveals immigration imprisonment for what it truly is. It's not a humane means of enforcing fair laws; it's an over-the-top reaction to a legal system designed to keep migrants in their place at the bottom of a social hierarchy that metes out favors and punishments according to race and class. The more privileged you already are, the more favored you will continue to be. Immigration prisons reveal the ugly, generations-old politics of exploiting segments of humanity. This isn't the first time, and it seems unlikely to be the last. But that doesn't make it any better.

Perhaps surprisingly, the Supreme Court has pointed in the direction of a more humane approach toward limiting imprisonment. Governmental action that "treat[s] members of the human race as nonhumans, as objects to be toyed with and discarded," the Court wrote in 1972, violate the Constitution's Cruel and Unusual Punishments Clause.[30] This principle, grounded in the Magna Carta, the famous thirteenth-century English legal document, and crystallized more clearly in the 1688 English Declaration of Rights, made its way into the Constitution as a means of protecting the "dignity of man."[31]

"You should be treated with dignity," David Rodriguez, who spent two and a half months inside a Houston immigration prison, insists. But what does it mean to treat people as human beings filled with an innate dignity? Not much, it would seem, given the state of imprisonment in the United States. In a series of lawsuits, people locked up in California's notoriously overcrowded, dangerous, and generally heinous prisons attempted to revive the moribund Cruel and Unusual Punishments Clause by arguing that they deserved a measure of dignity even as they atoned for their crimes. To their credit, the courts displayed a sympathetic ear and drew a line in the margins of acceptable imprisonment where no line had seemed to exist. Convicted offenders cannot be denied "life's necessities," concluded a specially impaneled three-judge trial court.[32] On appeal two years later, the Supreme Court added, "Prisoners retain the essence of human dignity inherent in all persons."[33] The specific problem of prison overcrowding that the Court addressed is fairly narrow, but the underlying dehumanization of prisoners is much broader.

For that reason, the Court's recognition that people don't stop being people when they find themselves behind bars is momentous. In breathing a sliver of life into the Constitution's dignity principle, the justices acknowledged that legal procedures can make life miserable, but they shouldn't be allowed to override the basic elements of human existence. In those legal decisions, courts, including the U.S. Supreme Court, declared that the acts that led people into prison are insufficient justification to deny them basic components of a dignified life. They can be imprisoned, but they can't be denied their humanity.

The twentieth-century philosopher Hannah Arendt would have agreed. A German Jew who survived Nazism by fleeing first to Paris, then to New York, Arendt's 1951 intellectual tour de force, *The Origins of Totalitarianism*, continues to set the standard for critiques of despotism's dangers. Rightly so, her focus was on Europeans who had been stripped of their citizenship before being stripped of their lives by Nazi forces and their allies. In writing broadly about totalitarianism, she highlighted the mundane features of systematized dehumanization. People stripped of law's protections were converted into "the scum of the earth," she wrote.[34] But she also described the law's potential to resurrect. "The same man who was in jail yesterday because of his mere presence in the world, who had no rights whatsoever and lived under threat of deportation . . . may become a full-fledged citizen because of a little theft," she added. "He is no longer the scum of the earth but important enough to be informed of all the details of the law under which he will be tried. He has become a respectable person."[35] So long as the law continues acknowledging a person's legitimate role in the community, she seemed to be saying, it will recognize the person's humanity. When the first ends, so too does the second.

Alone, neither federal courts' tepid embrace of human dignity nor Arendt's trenchant analysis is enough to end immigration imprisonment. Prisons in the United States remain teeming with people. But legal challenges to horrendous conditions inside California prisons provide a helpful example from which to resist immigration imprisonment by insisting on respect for migrants' inherent humanity. A politically charged sense of dignity must be at the core of that struggle. It is not enough to ask that immigration prisoners not be killed, starved, physically abused, or sexually assaulted. The Supreme Court's embrace of dignity is helpful, but too limited. Indeed, it must be because of the limitations inherent in legal proceedings. Courts of law are good venues for demanding that we treat each other according to the norms we have already agreed upon, but they are not particularly good venues for improving the conduct we demand of each other.

Instead, we should dream. Allison Crennen-Dunlap has summarized trends in Supreme Court decisions that enlarge the power of federal officials to detain migrants by reducing the oversight role that immigration judges play. According to her, "it seems then that the range of rights once thought possible for noncitizens has narrowed. Might the time be ripe to ask some bigger questions?"[36] In simply asking the question, Crennen-Dunlap answered it. The scale of the nation's immigration prison system continuously grows. The conditions of confinement seem impossible to improve. The faces of prisoners grow younger and more vulnerable. For all their differences, Democrats and Republicans regularly agree to support immigration prison practices. Instead of continuing to beat around the bush, it is important to inject into immigration conversations a more fundamental line of attack: it is time to abolish immigration prisons.

To deny some people core features of human existence simply because they lack governmental authorizations to cross certain lines marked on maps, lines that from time to time move or disappear, is to deny migrants their ability to realize their humanity. Forcing migrants to live under the constant threat of imprisonment tied to their immigration status means treating them as if they are workers and threats before they are people. "It's unreal the lengths they'll go to dehumanize," David Rodriguez told me, reflecting on his experience at the Houston immigration prison. To derail treatment of migrants as scum, as disposable, advocates need to insist that a dignified life includes the right to live with one's family, to flee danger, and work to sustain oneself. Legal battles can be a helpful adjunct, but ultimately this is a political fight about the future that is grounded in the past.

Throughout all this, somehow migrants and their families are expected to weather the storms of strong-armed policing. As if through superhuman powers, they are to put aside the trauma of imprisonment, the practical obstacles of being uprooted from their lives and their jobs. They are supposed to be exceptional human beings. We need to stop demanding that migrants be exceptional and instead embrace their ordinariness. Today's migrants are doing what people have done for millennia: moving from place to place in search of comfort, safety, adventure—all that makes life worth living. Indeed, in search of life itself. In the Christian tradition, trekking across the Earth begins with Adam and Eve's fall from grace. In Islam, it started with Muhammed's search for safety. In Judaism, it is central to the Jewish people's survival.

People don't wake up one morning and simply decide they will leave their homes, families, and communities. Leaving the place where people know you and you know others is never easy. This is as true for people living in poverty as it is for people suffering from violence. On their own, push factors like these, as scholars call reasons to leave, are rarely enough to get up and go. If they were, then everyone living near a richer destination would set off. And yet most Guatemalans don't head to Mexico, and most Mexicans don't head to the United States. The same goes for the United States, where there are few legal hurdles to state-to-state migration. Colorado, where I live, has the eighth best employment record in the country. Our southern neighbor, New Mexico, has the sixth worst. If money were sufficient reason to convince most people to move, we could expect an exodus north, but we don't see that. Like most people, most New Mexicans stay put.

Often, we think of migrants as foreign people who are coming to what is, for them, a foreign place. "They came into a strange land," the *New York Times* wrote in its 1954 celebration of Ellis Island's last day as a detention center. Unfamiliarity retains a powerful place in our collective imagination of migrants. But for many people, coming to the United States doesn't mean arriving unmoored. People come to the United States for specific reasons. Just like people are pushed away from home by unique factors, they are pulled toward their new home by preexisting relationships. The sociologist Saskia Sassen captured this idea brilliantly when she wrote that "migrations do not simply happen. They are produced. And migrations do not involve just any possible combination of countries. They are patterned."[37] In other words, migrants don't head to the United States randomly. They come here because it is a stable country with good job prospects and deep ties to key parts of the world. Around the United States, there are large, thriving communities of migrants from China, India, the Philippines, Mexico, and Central America. In places like California and Texas, this has been true for generations. In the new migrant destinations of the South and Midwest, migration has been commonplace for less time, but by now it is part of the lifeblood of many communities that have seen hard times. These are the ties that bind the United States to the rest of the world, and they are firm. In bilingual, bicultural, binational people like me, they are made real.

Over and over again, government officials ignore the over-
whelming human desire of people to improve their lot. During
the summer of 2014, the government of El Salvador distributed
a flashy cartoon called "El cuento del coyote" ("The Smuggler's
Tale"), in which a stereotypical bad guy—curved nose, sharpened teeth, and grimy clothes—locks children in a cage while a
boy's voice talks about being sold by a smuggler. "Protecting our
children is our responsibility," a grandmotherly type admon-
ishes.[38] Funded by the United States, the International Organization for Migration, and UNICEF, the cartoon apparently
didn't make much of a dent, because families and children keep
coming. And the United States keeps trying to scare them away.
Four years after the failed cartoon nightmare was released, Kevin
McAleenan, then the director of Customs and Border Protection, visited Guatemala to tout Trump administration efforts "to
provide accurate information so they won't make this dangerous
journey, where they face physical and sexual assault," according to
news reports.[39]

The anti-smuggling video and McAleenan's comments suggest
migrants don't know the risks of the journey north. In reality, migrants are simply responding to a greater desire to see their loved
ones and make a safe life for themselves and their families—to
live. Legal scholar Jennifer Chacón vividly captured the immense
power that the reasons for migration have and the limited sway
that imprisonment offers. "Would-be migrants who are undeterred by the very real and well-known threats of robbery, serious
violence, rape, sexual assault, and death in the desert in the course
of northward migration seem likely to give very little weight to the
possibility of criminal sanctions when deciding to undertake the
journey."[40] The evidence backs her up. In one survey of over six
hundred Mexican migrants, a mere fifty-five said law enforcement
efforts deterred them from coming. In another, Central American
migrants came even though roughly 80 percent were apprehended

by immigration officials at some point. People coming to reunite with family or in search of better job prospects are most likely to come no matter what obstacles government officials throw their way.[41]

Migrants are ordinary in another way. Like all of us, migrants mess up. On average, they commit less crime than do those of us born in the United States. Along the Southwest border, counties with large migrant populations "have significantly *lower* levels of lethal violence than non-border counties," the criminologist Jacob Stowell and his colleagues found.[42] The same goes for property crime.[43] It's true of Haitians in Miami, Asians in San Diego, and Mexicans in Chicago.[44] President Trump can bluster all he wants about gangs of migrants terrorizing our neighborhoods, but if what we want is safer cities and towns, we should recruit migrants. But less crime doesn't mean no crime. Some migrants steal, and others hurt people. Denying that reality is to hold migrants to an impossibly high bar. Politically, it's also a losing strategy. Pointing to exceptionally talented and saintly migrants as a model is a recipe for lumping mere mortals—that's most of us—into the category of undesirable arrivals. Let's stop sanctifying migrants and embrace the profound ordinariness that makes migrants, like citizens, human.

We also need to stop pretending that crime is a good indicator of moral worth. Having spent most of my adult life on college campuses, I am constantly reminded that we have all done things that are nothing worse than embarrassing and other things that are far worse. Sometimes regret begins to set in at the very moment, but we can't stop ourselves. On occasion, our transgressions cross the line from a moral failing to a crime. The stain of a criminal conviction doesn't make some people worse than people who have moved through life without a blemish. Often, criminal investigation, prosecution, and conviction reflect dumb luck or the indefensible bias of the U.S. criminal justice system.

Besides, the criminal justice system doesn't pretend to overlap perfectly with criminal activity. Most people who commit a crime in the United States aren't convicted. In fact, most violent crime and property crime isn't even reported to the police.[45] When police do get a call, they are not required to investigate every allegation, even if it's credible. They simply don't have the money to chase down every possible criminal. And when they do investigate, prosecutors don't have to turn to the courts for justice. They can define justice however they like. If that means trying to convict someone, so be it. If it means not trying, that's fine too. "A prosecutor," the Supreme Court wrote in 1982, has "broad discretion . . . to determine the societal interest in prosecution."[46] It might have clarified: "in prosecution *or not*."

When a prosecutor does go after someone, a conviction might have little to do with what the person actually did. First, plenty of innocent people are convicted. Thousands of people have had their convictions overturned, often thanks to belated use of DNA evidence. There is reason to believe that many more people have been wrongly convicted, but the courts are unfriendly toward claims of innocence. As Justice Antonin Scalia put it with the bitterness that was his trademark, "This Court has *never* held that the Constitution forbids the execution of a convicted defendant who has had a full and fair trial but is later able to convince a habeas court that he is 'actually' innocent."[47] Second, almost no one is convicted by trial. Nine out of ten people convicted admit their guilt through the "horse trading" process of negotiating pleas.[48] Often, people plead guilty because the risk of challenging the prosecutor is so high. Prosecutors routinely charge people with multiple crimes. The possibility of long prison stints gives defendants an incentive to admit their guilt to something less than what the prosecutor has charged—even if that means accepting punishment for something they didn't do.

Testifying before the Senate Judiciary Committee as his nomination to the Supreme Court teetered, Brett Kavanaugh defended himself against sexual assault allegations by saying, "all of us have probably done things we look back on in high school and regret or cringe a bit."[49] Cecilia Equihua would likely agree. She remembers her father, Francisco, who was held in multiple immigration prisons, as dedicated to his two daughters, but she doesn't deny that he let his garage be turned into a meth lab. Houston chef David Rodriguez doesn't deny that he hit two men with a baseball bat. Jerry Armijo doesn't deny falling into drugs when he returned from Iraq. And if he could understand the question, Diego Rivera Osorio, the little boy who turned three inside the Berks Family Residential Center in Pennsylvania, would probably admit that he and his mom didn't have the right stamps in their passports. As Kavanaugh suggested, most of us have some skeleton tucked into our past.

For people of color, especially those who aren't able to escape into the increased safety that wealth brings, the low points of our lives frequently become sticking points. Take a single week in September 2018, when President Trump's Justice Department issued a decision ratcheting up the immigration consequences of obstructing justice. This is an "aggravated felony," and, like all aggravated felonies, an obstruction of justice conviction brings mandatory imprisonment followed by almost-certain deportation.[50] That same week Trump's former campaign chairman Paul Manafort walked into a federal courthouse and pled guilty to obstruction of justice. For migrants, obstruction of justice comes with prison time, then mandatory detention by ICE, and finally deportation—all while an executive order signed by President Trump declares their presence in the United States "contrary to the national interest." For Manafort, obstruction of justice came with prison time and a supportive tweet from the president. If you are a well-placed, wealthy white man who lies to the FBI, you are a good guy who got nabbed by an overzealous Washington establishment. If you are an ordinary migrant, you are a danger to the richest, most powerful country on earth.

With luck and privilege playing such important roles in determining who gets convicted of a crime, it makes no sense to use criminal records to decide who is morally upstanding and who is not. The bottom line is that we are a mixed bag. Ending this double standard isn't as simple as ejecting President Trump from the White House. Congress and presidents from both major political parties have been tarring migrants for decades and supporting imprisonment as a catch-all response. When Ellen Knauff was forced to stay on Ellis Island, the Supreme Court said she was enjoying "temporary harborage" there. Three-quarters of a century later, the courts haven't budged. Immigration prisons have never been more widespread. If that is going to change, it won't be because the law demands it. It will be because people demand it.

of creative, impassioned courage: courage to discard what we in the United States do for what we should do. Whether blue-state Democrats or red-state Republicans, politicians support immigration prisons. They fan fears of migrants roaming the streets under the cloak of nighttime darkness. Migrants join gangs, President Obama said. Migrants behead, President Trump added. There is a little bit of truth and a ton of sensationalism in both fear-laced remarks.

Countering the dehumanizing spirit of the bipartisan embrace of immigration prisons needs to begin with a wholesale embrace of the imperfect humanity of migrants. Migrants are superheroes, I tell my students when they ask why Superman often appears in problems I have them work on in class. The most American of aliens definitely didn't ask the government's permission to crash into a Kansas farm before growing into a one-man paramilitary force with a penchant for violence. But migrants also commit crimes, cheat on their spouses, get mired in poverty, and lie about it. Migrants aren't imperfect because they aren't citizens. Migrants are imperfect because they are people. Just people.

Any political alliance with migrants requires embracing all of this. Not out of celebration for all that migrants do for citizens. Not because migrants boost our economy, pick our crops, clean our offices, care for our young, or energize our culture. We should embrace the imperfect humanity of migrants to celebrate that we are all strange creatures: migrants and citizens alike. "The point is . . . not to recognize ourselves in strangers, not to gloat in the comforting falsity that 'they are like us', but to recognize a stranger in ourselves," urges the philosopher Slavoj Žižek. Why? Because "we are all, in our own way, strange lunatics."[1]

Migrants aren't stunted versions of people like me born into my citizenship. They're not just people standing along the route that I traveled in utero. In this moment, in the context of one nation, I am the citizen, and others are not. But in another moment, things

CONCLUSION

With support from Washington to Willacy County, it seems that the future is bright for immigration prisons. In the days after Trump's election, private prison stock skyrocketed, suggesting that it is a good time to be in the business of locking up migrants. As a nation, our collective moral compass has swerved to the point that we no longer debate whether we should lock up children. Instead, detaining children with their mothers is offered as the humanitarian response to taking children from their parents. The nightmare of confining kids is now the official policy of the U.S. government. When that is our reality, then imaginations have already run wild.

If nightmares can become reality, why can't dreams? Instead of an immigration-law enforcement strategy afraid that migrants will pour into our churches and schools, onto our streets and our playgrounds, I imagine a different future. I imagine a future that looks more like United States history than United States present. I imagine a future in which immigration prisons do not exist. This is a long, winding road, and I do not pretend to have all the answers that could get us from here to there.

But I do know that the story of immigration prisons isn't a story about the righteousness of law. It's a story about politics. Politics always matters, but when it comes to immigration prisons, politics are everywhere. Combatting immigration prisons requires tackling politics with politics. It's past time to push back against the decades-old bipartisan politics of fear with a politics change. I am a U.S. citizen only because my mother migrated so that I wouldn't have to. And in another context, they change again. When I am not in the United States, I am the migrant, and others are the citizens. Whether we know it or not, whether we admit it or not, "we are all becoming migrants." [2] For that profoundly ordinary fact of human existence, none of us deserve to see the inside of a prison.

ACKNOWLEDGMENTS

This project would not have been possible without the immense assistance of many individuals. Some are mentioned in the text. Most are not for there are simply too many people upon whom my work builds.

My professional home at the University of Denver has provided me with expansive intellectual and financial support to carry this book from an idea to the finished product before you. Thanks to the generosity of the University of Denver Office of the Associate Provost for Research, the Hughes-Rudd Research and Development Committee, and the College of Law, I was able to conduct the research needed to bring this book to life. My students have been invaluable inspirations as they challenged me to think deeper and clearer about immigration prisons. I am especially indebted to Allison Crennen-Dunlap, the first person to read a complete draft of this manuscript and the last to go easy on me about any oversights.

Along the way, I have spoken with activists, advocates, and academics who have sharpened my understanding of the role that prisons occupy in modern-day immigration policing. Lauren Dasse fights in Arizona; Adriel Orozco, Emma Kahn, and Arifa Raza in New Mexico; Cecilia Equihua in Los Angeles; Julia Braker in Oregon; and Sharon Phillips in New York. Ming Chen and Elizabeth Escobedo kindly allowed me to share parts of this project with their students. Meanwhile, my brothers, Raúl and Carlos, have been my immigration-lawyer guides at our family law firm, García & García Attorneys at Law.

Without my colleague and partner, Margaret, I would not have had the time or energy for this book. For that, I am forever indebted.

NOTES

Introduction

1. Anthony Orozco, *Attorney Hails Mother and Son's Release from Berks County Residential Center*, Reading Eagle (August 11, 2017), https://www.read ingeagle.com/news/article/attorney-hails-mother-and-sons-release-from-berk -county-residential-center; Laura Benshoff, *Judge Frees Mom, Toddler from Berks Immigrant Detention Center After 22 Months*, WHYY (August 8, 2017), https:// whyy.org/articles/judge-frees-mom-toddler-from-berks-immigrant-detention -center-after-22-months-confinement.

2. Osorio-Martinez v. Attorney General, 893 F.3d 153, 178 (3d Cir. 2018).

3. Edafe Okporo, Bed 26: A Memoir of an African Man's Asylum in the United States 14, 19 (2018).

4. Admin. Office of the U.S. Courts, Federal Judicial Business, Fiscal Year 2018, U.S. District Courts-Petty Offense Defendants Disposed of, by U.S. Magistrate Judges, by Nature of Offense, During the 12-Month Period Ending September 30, 2018, 1 tbl.M-2 (2019), https://www.uscourts.gov/sites/default/files /data_tables/jb_m2_0930.2018.pdf; Admin. Office of the U.S. Courts, Federal Judicial Business, Fiscal Year 2018, U.S. District Courts-Criminal Defendants Disposed of, by Type of Disposition and Offense, During the 12-Month Period Ending September 30, 2018, 3 tbl.D-4 (2019), https://www.uscourts.gov/sites /default/files/data_tables/jb_d4_0930.2018.pdf.

5. Cecilia Equihua, *My Father's Story—and Why Congress Should Listen*, Huffington Post (October 16, 2015), https://www.huffingtonpost.com/cecilia -equihua/my-fathers-storyand-why-cb8312402.html.

6. Judith A. Greene et al., Indefensible: A Decade of Mass Incarceration of Migrants Prosecuted for Crossing the Border 129 (2016).

7. U.S. Immigr. & Naturalization Serv., 1996 Statistical Yearbook of the Immigr. and Naturalization Serv. 175 tbl.60, 183 tbl.65 (1997).

8. Admin. Office of the U.S. Courts, 1978 Ann. Rep. of the Director for the Twelve-Month Period Ending June 30, 1978, at 121 tbl.54 (n.d.).

9. Admin. Office of the U.S. Courts, Judicial Bus. 1997 Ann. Rep. 188 tbl.D-2.

10. César Cuauhtémoc García Hernández, *Pretrial Immigration Prisoner Trends, Part I*, crimmigration.com (September 15, 2016, 4:00 AM), http://crim migration.com/2016/09/15/pretrial-immigration-prisoner-trends-1994-2012.

11. César Cuauhtémoc García Hernández, *Immigration Prison Population Since 1990s*, crimmigration.com (September 19, 2017, 4:00 AM), http://crimmi gration.com/2017/09/19/immigration-prison-population-since-1990s.

12. Mark Dow, American Gulag: Inside U.S. Immigration Prisons 8 (2004).

13. Asa Hutchinson, *Keynote Address*, 59 Admin. L. Rev. 533, 541 (2007).

14. Alexandra La Golosa, *About Eloy*, IMM-Print.com (October 18, 2016), https://medium.com/imm-print/the-poems-of-alexandra-la-golosa-82225f7502 c1#.hrsmyqo6u.

15. Guillermo Cantor, *Hieleras (Iceboxes) in the Rio Grande Valley Sector: Lengthy Detention, Deplorable Conditions, and Abuse in CBP Holding Cells* 15 (2015).

16. Press Release, ICE, Denver-area ICE Detainee Passes Away at Local Hospital (December 4, 2017), https://www.ice.gov/news/releases/denver-area-ice-de tainee-passes-away-local-hospital.

17. Letter from Jared Polis, Member of Congress, to Thomas Homan, Acting Director, ICE 2 (June 20, 2018), https://polis.house.gov/uploadedfiles/062018 _ltr_aurora_detention_facility.pdf.

18. Memorandum from Jennifer M. Fenton, Assistant Director, Immigration and Customs Enforcement, to Matthew Albence, Executive Associate Director, Enforcement and Removal Operations, Findings—Death of ICE Detainee Kamyar Samimi 2 (May 22, 2018).

19. O'lone v. Estate of Shabazz, 482 U.S. 342, 354 (1987) (Brennan, J., dissenting).

20. U.S. Dep't of Homeland Security, Homeland Security Advisory Council, Rep. of the Subcommittee on Privatized Immigration Detention Facilities 6 tbl.1 (2016).

21. Erik Larson, *Captive Company*, Inc. Magazine (June 1, 1988), at 87, 88.

22. Krsna Avila et al., Immigrant Legal Resource Center, The Rise of Sanctuary: Getting Local Officers Out of the Business of Deportations in the Trump Era 9 (2018).

23. Molly Smith, *Family of Veteran Detained by ICE Pleads for his Release*, The Monitor (February 26, 2019).

1: Laying the Groundwork

1. Gerald L. Neuman, *The Lost Century of American Immigration Law (1776–1875)*, 93 Colum. L. Rev. 1833, 1842 (1993).

2. *Id.* at 1850–51 (discussing Smith v. City of Boston, 48 U.S. 283 (1849)).

3. *Id.* at 1866–69.

4. David Scott FitzGerald and David Cook-Martín, Culling the Masses: The Democratic Origins of Racist Immigration Policy in the Americas 90–91 (2014).

5. Nayan Shah, Contagious Divides: Epidemics and Race in San Francisco's Chinatown 20, 25 (2001).

6. *Id.* at 35.

7. Charles J. McClain, In Search of Equality: The Chinese Struggle Against Discrimination in Nineteenth-Century America 12–28 (1994).

8. Erika Lee, At America's Gates: Chinese Immigration During the Exclusion Era, 1882–1943, at 39 (2003).

9. Mary Roberts Coolidge, Chinese Immigration 283 (1909) (divinity student); Torrie Hester, Deportation: The Origins of U.S. Policy 67–68 (2017) (grocer).

10. 26 Stat. 1084, ch. 551, § 11 (1891).

11. Robert Eric Barde, Immigration at the Golden Gate: Passenger Ships, Exclusion and Angel Island 70 (2008).

12. Coolidge, *supra* note 9, at 299.

13. Roger Daniels, *No Lamps Were Lit for Them: Angel Island and the Historiography of Asian American Immigration*, 17 J. Am. Ethnic History 3, 4 (1997).

14. Coolidge, *supra* note 9, at 300.

15. *Id.*

16. Barde, *supra* note 11, at 70.

17. *Id.* at 71.

18. Coolidge, *supra* note 9, at 321.

19. Daniel Wilsher, Immigration Detention: Law, History, Politics 12 (2012).

20. Act of March 3, 1891, ch. 551, § 8, 26 Stat. 1084, 1085.

21. Act of March 3, 1893, ch. 206, § 5, 27 Stat. 569, 570.

22. Hubert Howe Bancroft, History of California, vol. 7, 1860–1890, at 336–37 (1890).

23. Robert Barde & Gustavo J. Bobonis, *Detention at Angel Island: First Empirical Evidence*, 30 Soc. Sci. History 103, 107 tbl.1 (2006).

24. Barde and Bobonis, *supra* note 23, at 109 tbl.2 (reporting 5,605 arrivals to Angel Island in 1913); Dep't of Commerce, U.S. Census Bureau, Stat. Abstract of the United States, 1919, 103 tbl.72 (1920) (reporting 14,844 arrivals at the San Francisco port of entry in 1913, including 8,935 non–United States citizens).

25. Barde and Bobonis, *supra* note 23, at 109 tbl.2.

26. *Id.* at 121, 124.

27. Robert Barde, *An Alleged Wife: One Immigrant in the Chinese Exclusion Era*, 36 Prologue 24 (2004).

28. Daniels, *supra* note 13, at 5.

29. Wilsher, *supra* note 19, at 16; National Park Service, *U.S. Immigration Statistics: Immigration Station at Ellis Island, NY*, https://www.nps.gov/elis/learn/education/upload/Statistics.pdf.

30. Richard Polenberg, Fighting Faiths: The Abrams Case, The Supreme Court, and Free Speech 10 (1987).

31. Elizabeth Hull, Without Justice for All: The Constitutional Rights of Aliens 18 (1985).

32. Patrick Ettinger, Imaginary Lines: Border Enforcement and the Origins of Undocumented Immigration, 1882–1930, at 147 (2009).

33. Daniel Kanstroom, Deportation Nation: Outsiders in American History 149–50 (2007).

34. Emma Goldman, Living My Life, Vol. II 717 (Dover ed. 1970) (1931).

35. Christian G. Fritz, *A Nineteenth Century "Habeas Corpus Mill": The Chinese Before the Federal Courts in California*, 32 Am. J. L. Hist. 347, 348 (1988).

36. *Id.* at 368.

37. Wong Wing v. United States, 163 U.S. 228, 235 (1896).

38. Knauff v. Shaugnessy, 338 U.S. 537, 550 (1950) (Jackson, J., dissenting).

39. Ellen Raphael Knauff, The Ellen Knauff Story 9 (1952).

40. Mark Dow, American Gulag: Inside U.S. Immigration Prisons 6 (2004).

41. *Knauff*, 338 U.S. at 539–40 (majority opinion).

42. *Id.* at 544.

43. *See, e.g.*, Castro v. DHS, 835 F.3d 422, 443 (3d Cir. 2016).

44. Charles D. Weisselberg, *The Exclusion and Detention of Aliens: Lessons from the Lives of Ellen Knauff and Ignatz Mezei*, 143 U. Pa. L. Rev. 933, 958 & nn.123–26 (1995).

45. *Matter of Ellen Raphael Knauff*, A-6937471 (BIA Aug. 29, 1951) (unpublished), *reprinted in* Ellen Raphael Knauff, The Ellen Knauff Story app.16, at 245 (1952).

46. Shaugnessy v. Mezei, 345 U.S. 206, 208 (1953).

47. *Id.* at 213.

48. *Id.* at 220 (Jackson, J., dissenting).

49. *Id.*

50. *Id.* at 226.

51. Carlson v. Landon, 342 U.S. 524, 538 (1952).

52. Rana Mitter, Forgotten Ally: China's World War II, 1937–1945, at 5 (2013).

53. FitzGerald & Cook-Martín, *supra* note 4, at 29.

54. Bill Ong Hing, *The Immigration Act of 1952, in* Anti-Immigration in the United States: A Historical Encyclopedia, Vol. 1, at 791, 792 (Kathleen R. Arnold ed., 2011).

55. Henry N. Rosenfield, *The Prospects for Immigration Amendments*, 21 Law & Contemp. Probs. 401, 405 (1956).

56. FitzGerald & Cook-Martín, *supra* note 4, at 29.

2: On the Prison's Edge

1. Benjamin Heber Johnson, Revolution in Texas: How a Forgotten Rebellion and Its Bloody Suppression Turned Mexicans into Americans 119 (2005).

2. William D. Carrigan & Clive Webb, *The Lynching of Persons of Mexican Origin or Descent in the United States, 1848 to 1928*, 37 J. of Soc. Hist. 411, 413–14 (2003).

3. Richard Delgado, *The Law of the Noose: A History of Latino Lynching*, 44 Harv. C.R.-C.L. L. Rev. 297, 299–300 (2009).

4. Carrigan & Webb, *supra* note 2, at 418.

5. Mae M. Ngai, Impossible Subjects: Illegal Aliens and the Making of Modern America 143 (2004).

6. Manuel García y Griego, *The Importation of Mexican Contract Laborers to the United States, 1942–1964, in* Between Two Worlds: Mexican Immigrants in the United States 45, 61 (David G. Gutiérrez ed., 1996).

7. Cybelle Fox, Three Worlds of Relief: Race, Immigration, and the American Welfare State from the Progressive Era to the New Deal 243 (2012).

8. John D. Gould, *European Inter-Continental Emigration: The Road Home: Return Migration from the U.S.A.*, 9 J. of European Econ. History 41, 57 tbl. 2 (1980).

9. Ngai, *supra* note 5, at 262 & n.120.

10. *Id.* at 261 (2004).

11. Arthur C. Helton, *The Legality of Detaining Refugees in the United States*, 14 NYU Rev. L. & Soc. Change 353, 355 (1986).

12. Mark Dow, American Gulag: Inside U.S. Immigration Prisons 7 (2004).

13. *Ellis Island Ends Alien Processing*, New York Times, November 13, 1954, at 20.

14. Note, *Wetbacks: Can the States Act to Curb Illegal Entry?*, 6 Stan. L. Rev. 287, 287 (1954).

15. Kelly Lytle Hernández, *The Crimes and Consequences of Illegal Immigration: A Cross-Border Examination of Operation Wetback, 1943 to 1954*, 37 Western Hist. Q. 421, 441–42 (2006).

16. Gilbert Paul Carrasco, *Latinos in the United States: Invitation and Exile*, *in* Immigrants Out! The New Nativism and the Anti-Immigrant Impulse in the United States 190, 197 (Juan F. Perea ed., 1997).

17. Hernández, *supra* note 15, at 443.

18. Carrasco, *supra* note 16, at 107.

19. *Ellis Island Ends Alien Processing*, New York Times (November 13, 1954), at 20.

20. Philip L. Martin, Promise Unfulfilled: Unions, Immigration, and the Farm Workers 48 (2003).

21. Joseph Nevins, Operation Gatekeeper and Beyond: The War on "Illegals" and the Remaking of the U.S.-Mexico Boundary app. F, at 227 (2001).

22. INS v. Delgado, 466 U.S. 210, 218 (1984).

23. *Id.* at 218, 219.

24. INS v. Lopez-Mendoza, 468 U.S. 1032, 1035 (1984).

25. *Id.*

26. *Id.* at 1040.

27. *Id.* at 1050.

28. Matthew Garcia & Mario Sifuentez, *The Foundations of Modern Farm Worker Unionism: From UFW to PCUN, in* Labor Rising: The Past and Future of Working People in America 253, 255–56 (Richard A. Greenwald & Daniel Katz eds., 2012).

3: The Resurgence of Immigration Prisons

1. A Nation Without Prisons: Alternatives to Incarceration 4–5 (Calvert R. Dodge ed., 1975).

2. Milton G. Rector, *Introduction* to A Nation Without Prisons: Alternatives to Incarceration xvii, xvii (Calvert R. Dodge ed., 1975).

3. Corrs. Task Force, Nat'l Advisory Comm'n on Criminal Justice Standards and Goals, *Major Institutions, in* A Nation Without Prisons: Alternatives to Incarceration 3, 22 (Calvert R. Dodge ed., 1975).

4. Loïc Wacquant, Prisons of Poverty 135 (expanded ed. 2009).

5. Angela Y. Davis, Are Prisons Obsolete? 10 (2003).

6. Dan Baum, *Legalize It All: How to Win the War on Drugs,* Harper's (April 2016), https://harpers.org/archive/2016/04/legalize-it-all/.

7. Katherine Beckett, Making Crime Pay: Law and Order in Contemporary American Politics 23, 55, 62 (1997).

8. David J. Garland, The Culture of Control: Crime and Social Order in Contemporary Society 10, 136, 154 (2001).

9. C-SPAN, *1996: Hillary Clinton on "Superpredators,"* YouTube (February 25, 2016), https://www.youtube.com/watch?v=j0uCrA7ePno.

10. Jonathan Simon, Governing Through Crime: How the War on Crime Transformed American Democracy and Created a Culture of Fear 76 (2007).

11. George J. Kelling & James Q. Wilson, *Broken Windows: The Police and Neighborhood Safety,* Atlantic Monthly, March 1982, at 29.

12. Simon, *supra* note 10, at 129–30.

13. 133 Cong. Rec. 28,840 (1987) (statement of Rep. Smith).

14. Stephanie J. Silverman, *Immigration Detention in America: A History of Its Expansion and a Study of Its Significance* 10 (Univ. of Oxford, Working Paper No. 80, 2010).

15. Jenna M. Loyd & Alison Mountz, Boats, Borders, and Bases: Race, the Cold War, and the Rise of Migration Detention in the United States 92–93, 98 (2018).

16. William M. LeoGrande, Our Own Backyard: The United States in Central America, 1977–1992, 448 (1998).

17. American Baptist Churches v. Meese, 712 F. Supp. 756, 765 (N.D. Cal. 1989).

18. Oscar Martinez et al., *Tin-Cup Gangs of El Salvador,* New York Times, at A1 (November 20, 2016); U.S. Dep't of Homeland Security, Immigration and Customs Enforcement, *Treasury Department, HIS Sanction Significant Members of MS-13 Gang,* https://www.ice.gov/news/releases/treasury-department-hsi-sanction-significant-members-ms-13-gang (June 4, 2013).

19. David Bacon, Illegal People: How Globalization Creates Migration and Criminalizes Migrants 60–64 (2008).

20. Joseph Nevins, Operation Gatekeeper and Beyond: The War on "Illegals" and the Remaking of the U.S.-Mexico Boundary app. F, at 227 (2001).

21. Pima County Office of the Medical Examiner, Annual Report 2016, at 31, http://webcms.pima.gov/UserFiles/Servers/Server_6/File/Government/Medical%20Examiner/Resources/Annual-Report-2016.pdf.

22. Douglas Massey et al., *Why Border Enforcement Backfired*, 121 Am. J. Soc. 1557, 1557–58, 1578, 1588 (2016).

23. Hoffman Plastic Compounds, Inc. v. NLRB, 535 U.S. 137, 151–52 (2002).

24. Massey et al., *supra* note 22, at 1581; Julie A. Phillips & Douglas S. Massey, *The New Labor Market: Immigrants and Wages After IRCA*, 36 Demography 233, 243 (1999).

25. Nielsen v. Preap, 139 S. Ct. 954, 968 (2019).

26. *Id.* at 959.

27. Immigration Act of 1990, Pub. L. No. 101-649, § 507, 104 Stat. 4978, 5050–51.

28. Margaret H. Taylor, *The 1996 Immigration Act: Detention and Related Issues*, 74 Interpreter Releases 209 (1997).

29. Matter of Truong, 22 I&N Dec. 1090 (BIA 1999).

30. *Detention of Aliens in Bureau of Prisons Facilities: Hearing Before the Subcomm. on Courts, Civil Liberties & the Admin. of Justice of the H. Comm. on the Judiciary*, 97th Cong. 1–3 (1982).

31. U.S. Dep't of Justice, Off. of the Inspector Gen., The September 11 Detainees: A Review of the Treatment of Aliens Held on Immigration Charges in Connection with the Investigation of the September 11 Attacks 12 (2003).

32. *Id.* at 111–15.

33. César Cuauhtémoc García Hernández, *ICE Transitioned from Obama to Trump with Record High Daily Detention Population*, crimmigration.com (April 3, 2018, 12:30 AM), http://crimmigration.com/2018/04/03/ice-transitioned-from-obama-to-trump-with-record-high-daily-detention-population.

34. United States v. Roblero-Solis, 588 F.3d 692, 700 (9th Cir. 2009).

35. Ingrid V. Eagly, *Prosecuting Immigration*, 104 Nw. U. L. Rev. 1281, 1351 (2010).

36. Sioban Albiol et al., *Re-Interpreting Postville: A Legal Perspective*, 2 Depaul J. for Soc. Just. 31, 33, 39 (2008).

37. Erik Camayd-Freixas, *Interpreting After the Largest ICE Raid in US History: A Personal Account* 2, 11 (2008).

38. Hamed Aleaziz, *The Rise of the ICE Official Who Said Detention Was "More Like Summer Camp,"* BuzzFeed News (August 7, 2018), https://www

.buzzfeednews.com/article/hamedaleaziz/under-trump-official-who-called-ice
-detention-more-like.

39. Tanya Golash-Boza, *The Immigration Industrial Complex: Why We En-force Immigration Policies Destined to Fail*, 3 Soc. Compass 295, 296 (2009).

4: The Immigration Prison Archipelago

1. *Federal Building, New York, NY*, U.S. Gen. Serv. Admin., https://www.gsa.gov/historic-buildings/federal-building-new-york-ny#significance (last visited November 14, 2018).

2. Dhine v. Slattery, 3 F.3d 613, 619 (2nd Cir. 1993).

3. Jackie Rothenberg, *INS Releases Ethiopian Jew After 9 Years Behind Bars*, New York Post (May 24, 1999); Alisa Solomon, *The Prison on Varick Street*, New York Times (June 11, 1994), at A21.

4. U.S. Dep't of Homeland Security, Immigration and Customs Enforcement, Office of Detention Oversight Compliance Inspection: Enforcement and Removal Operations 1 (2012), https://www.ice.gov/doclib/foia/odo-compliance-inspections/eloy-dtn-ctr_eloy-AZ_july10-12_2012.pdf.

5. *About the Artesia Center*, Fed. Law Enforcement Training Centers, https://www.fletc.gov/about-artesia-center.

6. Anonymous, *What We Endured in Family Detention*, New York Times (June 26, 2018), at A23.

7. Letter from Scott Allen & Pamela McPherson to Hon. Charles E. Grassley et al. at 3–4 (July 17, 2018); Scott A. Allen & Pamela McPherson, *We Warned DHS That a Migrant Child Could Die in U.S. Custody*, Washington Post (December 19, 2018), https://www.washingtonpost.com/outlook/2018/12/19/we-warned-dhs-that-migrant-child-could-die-us-custody-now-one-has.

8. Julia Braker, *Declaration of Julia Braker*, 2 (August 15, 2014), https://www.aclu.org/files/assets/Declaratoin%20of%20Julia%20Braker_red.pdf.

9. Dep't of Homeland Security, Report of the DHS Advisory Committee on Family Residential Centers 38, 43 (2016).

10. Lutheran Immigration and Refugee Services & Women's Refugee Comm'n, Locking Up Family Values, Again 9 (2014).

11. *Id.* at 6 (2014).

12. Dora Schriro, Dep't of Homeland Security, Immigration and Customs Enforcement, Immigration Detention Overview and Recommendations 2 (2009).

13. César Cuauhtémoc García Hernández, *Prison Reform's Blind Spot*, crim migration.com (July 23, 2015, 4:00 AM), http://crimmigration.com/2015/07/23 /prison-reforms-blind-spot.

14. Reis Thebault, *How a Flight Attendant from Texas Ended Up in an ICE Detention Center for Six Weeks*, Washington Post (March 23, 2019), https:// www.washingtonpost.com/immigration/2019/03/23/how-flight-attendant-texas -ended-up-an-ice-detention-center-six-weeks.

15. 8 U.S.C. § 1158(a) (2012).

16. Alex Garcia-Ditta, *"She Lives in Fear," Not in El Salvador, but in Texas Detention*, Texas Observer, May 10, 2016, https://www.texasobserver.org/sexual -abuse-karnes-immigrant-detention.

17. Dep't. of Health & Human Services, Administration for Children & Families, Office of Refugee Resettlement, Annual Report to Congress Fiscal Year 2016, at 51 tbl.25 (2016); Dep't. of Health & Human Services, Administration for Children & Families, Office of Refugee Resettlement, Annual Report to Congress Fiscal Year 2008, at 61 (2011); Dep't. of Health & Human Services, Administration for Children & Families, Office of Refugee Resettlement, Facts and Data, Referrals, https://www.acf.hhs.gov/orr/about/ucs/facts-and-data (last visited June 12, 2019).

18. Emma Kaufman, *Segregation by Citizenship*, 132 Harvard Law Review 1379, 1404, 1416 (2019); Fed. Bureau of Prisons, Contract Prisons, https://www .bop.gov/about/facilities/contract_facilities.jsp (last visited June 10, 2019).

19. Schriro, *supra* note 12, at 4.

20. Malik Ndaula & Debbie Satyal, *Rafiu's Story: An American Immigrant Nightmare, in* Keeping Out the Other: A Critical Introduction to Immigration Enforcement Today 241, 250 (David C. Brotherton & Philip Kretsedemas eds., 2008).

21. In re Gault, 387 U.S. 1, 27 (1967) (internal citations omitted).

22. Caitlin Patler, The Economic Impacts of Long-Term Immigration Detention in Southern California 3–4 (2015).

23. *ICE Workplace Raids: Their Impact on U.S. Children, Families and Communities: Hearing Before the Subcomm. on Workforce Protections of the H. Comm. on Education and Labor*, 110th Cong. 23 (2008) (statement of Kathryn M. Gibney, Principal, San Pedro Elementary School, San Rafael, California).

24. Heather Koball et al., Health and Social Service Needs of US-Citizen Children with Detained or Deported Immigrant Parents 5 (2015).

25. Kalina Brabeck & Qingwen Xu, *The Impact of Detention and Deportation on Latino Immigrant Children and Families: A Quantitative Exploration*, 32 Hispanic J. of Behav. Sci. 341, 355 (2010).

26. Randy Capps et al., Paying the Price: The Impact of Immigration Raids on America's Children 36–37, 47 (2007).

27. Office of the Inspector Gen., Dep't of Homeland Sec., Removals Involving Illegal Alien Parents of United States Citizen Children 4, 6 fig. 2 (2009).

28. Nina Rabin, *Unseen Prisoners: A Report on Women in Immigration Detention Facilities in Arizona*, 23 Geo. Imm. L.J. 695, 737 (2009).

5: The Good Immigrant vs. the Bad Immigrant

1. Greg Morago, *Tout Suite Coffee Shop/Bakery Is Downtown's "It" Hangout*, Houston Chronicle, October 17, 2014, http://www.houstonpress.com/news/local-chef-wrongly-held-in-immigrant-detention-center-for-two-months-8101913.

2. 22 C.F.R. § 40.21(a)(1) (1999).

3. Jordan v. DeGeorge, 341 U.S. 223, 233–34 (1951) (Jackson, J., dissenting).

4. Leif Reigstad, *Local Chef Wrongly Held in Immigrant Detention Center for Two Months*, Houston Press, January 28, 2016, http://www.houstonpress.com/news/local-chef-wrongly-held-in-immigrant-detention-center-for-two-months-8101913.

5. Harriet Beecher Stowe, *The Minister's Wooing, in* Three Novels: Uncle Tom's Cabin, The Minister's Wooing, & Oldtown Folks 521, 576 (Library of America 1982).

6. Ronald Reagan, Election Eve Address: A Vision for America (November 3, 1980), https://www.reaganlibrary.gov/11-3-80.

7. President Ronald Reagan, Farewell Address to the Nation (January 11, 1989), http://www.presidency.ucsb.edu/ws/index.php?pid=29650.

8. President Barack Obama, Remarks by the President at the 50th Anniversary of the Selma Montgomery Marches (March 7, 2015), https://obamawhitehouse.archives.gov/the-press-office/2015/03/07/remarks-president-50th-anniversary-selma-montgomery-marches.

9. Lawrence Mishel & Jessica Schieder, Economic Policy Institute, CEO Compensation Surged in 2017, at 12 fig. C (August 16, 2018).

10. Kayla Fontenot et al., U.S. Census Bureau, Income and Poverty in the United States: 2017, at 11 (2018).

11. INA § 212(a)(2)(h), 8 U.S.C. § 1182(a)(2)(h) (2012); INA § 237(a)(2)(B)(i), 8 U.S.C. § 1227(a)(2)(B)(i) (2012).

12. Carachuri-Rosendo v. Holder, 560 U.S. 563, 574 (2010).

13. Mellouli v Lynch, 135 S. Ct. 1980, 1985 (2015).

14. Padilla v. Kentucky, 559 U.S. 356, 360 (2010) (internal quotations and citations omitted).

15. President Donald Trump (@realDonaldTrump), Twitter (October 29, 2018, 8:41 AM), https://twitter.com/realDonaldTrump/status/1056919064906 469376.

16. German Lopez, *Trump: After Mollie Tibbetts's Murder, "We Need the Wall,"* Vox (Aug. 23, 2018, 10:00 AM), https://www.vox.com/policy-and-politics /2018/8/23/17771318/trump-mollie-tibbett-immigration.

17. Mladen Dolar, *Who Is the Victim?, in* The Final Countdown: Europe, Refugees and the Left 67, 70 (Jela Krečič ed., 2017).

18. Emily Ryo, *Detained: A Study of Immigration Bond Hearings*, 50 Law & Soc'y Rev. 117, 119 (2016).

19. Julianne Hing, *Who Are Those 'Gangbangers' Obama's So Proud of Deporting?*, Colorlines (October 17, 2012, 10:11 AM), https://www.colorlines.com /articles/who-are-those-gangbangers-obamas-so-proud-deporting.

20. César Cuauhtémoc García Hernández, *Attorney General Delivers Fiery Speech in Defense of the Status Quo*, crimmigration.com (April 11, 2017, 3:13 PM), http://crimmigration.com/2017/04/11/attorney-general-delivers-fiery-speech -in-defense-of-the-status-quo.

21. *Release of Criminal Detainees by U.S. Immigration and Customs Enforcement: Policy or Politics?: Hearing Before the H. Comm. on the Judiciary*, 113th Cong. 12 (2013) (statement of John Morton, Director, U.S. Immigration and Customs Enforcement), https://www.hsdl.org/?view&did=737980.

22. *Id.* at 3 (statement of Rep. Bob Goodlatte, Chairman, H. Comm. on the Judiciary).

23. U.S. Dep't of Homeland Security, *DHS Statement on Tragic Death of Minor at Border* (December 14, 2018), https://www.facebook.com/homelandsecurity /posts/2256926350986655.

24. Patricia Sulbarán Lovera, *Felipe Gómez-Alonzo, el niño de Guatemala que murió persiguiendo el sueño americano*, BBC Mundo (March 17, 2019), https:// www.bbc.com/mundo/noticias-america-latina-47584393.

25. *See* Kawashima v. Holder, 565 U.S. 478, 480 (2012). Regarding their sentences, see Petitioner's Opening Brief, Kawashima v. Gonzales, 503 F.3d 997 (9th Cir. 2007) (No. 04-74313), 2005 WL 2106003, at *6.

26. Press Release, Congressman Steve King, King Introduces "Kate's Law" in the 115th Congress (January 6, 2017), https://steveking.house.gov/media-center/press-releases/king-introduces-kate-s-law-in-the-115th-congress.

27. Kate's Law, H.R. 3004, 115th Cong. (2017).

28. President Donald Trump (@realDonaldTrump), Twitter (July 13, 2015, 3:15 AM), https://twitter.com/realDonaldTrump/status/620672963499675648.

29. Donald J. Trump, Republican National Convention Nomination Acceptance Speech (July 21, 2016), https://www.politico.com/story/2016/07/full-transcript-donald-trump-nomination-acceptance-speech-at-rnc-225974.

30. Press Release, Sen. Dianne Feinstein, Feinstein Calls on San Francisco to Join DHS Immigration Program (July 7, 2015), https://www.feinstein.senate.gov/public/index.cfm/press-releases?ID=12DF46AD-0787-4083-934B-857B64ED6D23.

31. Knauff v. Shaughnessy, 338 U.S. 537, 540, 547 (1950).

32. *Id.* at 551 (Jackson, J., dissenting).

33. Shaughnessy v. Mezei, 345 U.S. 206, 208–09 (1953).

34. *Id.* at 215.

35. Andrea Gómez Cervantes et al., *"Humane" Immigration Enforcement and Latina Immigrants in the Detention Complex*, 12 Feminist Criminology 269, 278–79 (2017).

36. INA § 236(c), 8 U.S.C. § 1226(c) (2012).

37. INA § 276(b), 8 U.S.C. § 1326(b) (2012).

38. Black Alliance for Just Immigration, The State of Black Immigrants: Part I: A Statistical Portrait of Black Immigrants in the United States 10–11 (2016).

39. Black Alliance for Just Immigration, The State of Black Immigrants: Part II: Black Immigrants in the Mass Criminalization System 26 (2016).

40. INA § 208(a)(1), 8 U.S.C. § 1158(a)(1).

41. Alex Kuczynski, *Melania Trump's American Dream*, Harper's Bazaar, January 6, 2016, https://www.harpersbazaar.com/culture/features/a13529/melania-trump-interview-0216.

42. Dora Schriro, Dep't of Homeland Security, Immigration and Customs Enforcement, Immigration Detention Overview and Recommendations 4 (2009).

43. Nat'l Immigrant Justice Ctr., Invisible in Isolation: The Use of Segregation and Solitary Confinement in Immigration Detention 18 (2012).

6: The Money

1. KOB.com Web Staff, *Prison in Cibola County to Close in October* (August 2, 2016), https://www.privateci.org/new_mexico.htm.

2. Seth Freed Wessler, *Federal Officials Ignored Years of Internal Warnings About Deaths at Private Prisons*, The Nation (June 15, 2016), https://www.thenation.com/article/federal-officials-ignored-years-of-internal-warnings-about-deaths-at-private-prisons.

3. Seth Freed Wessler, *The Feds Will Shut Down the Troubled Private Prison in "Nation" Investigation*, The Nation (August 15, 2016), https://www.thenation.com/article/feds-will-shut-down-troubled-private-prison-in-nation-investigation.

4. U.S. Dep't of Just., Office of the Insp. Gen., Review of the Federal Bureau of Prisons' Monitoring of Contract Prisons ii (August 2016).

5. Uriel J. Garcia, *Western N.M. Communities Brace for Prison's Closure*, Santa Fe New Mexican (September 3, 2016), http://www.santafenewmexican.com/news/local_news/western-n-m-communities-brace-for-prison-s-closure/article_34b2c6af-1cd8-5e1b-b44e-b0402c69de8d.html.

6. Press Release, Management & Training Corporation, *MTC Signs Contract with ICE to Operate Detention Facility in Raymondville* (July 18, 2018), https://www.mtctrains.com/wp-content/uploads/2018/07/MTC-TO-OPERATE-FACILITY-IN-RAYMONDVILLE.pdf.

7. Jeremy Raff, *"So What? Maybe It Is a Concentration Camp,"* The Atlantic (February 23, 2018), https://www.theatlantic.com/politics/archive/2018/02/how-joe-arpaio-inspired-the-immigration-crackdown/554027.

8. Mark Noferi & Robert Koulish, *The Immigration Detention Risk Assessment*, 29 Geo. Immigr. L.J. 45, 47–48 (2015).

9. Robert S. Kahn, Other People's Blood: U.S. Immigration Prisons in the Reagan Decade 151–52 (1996).

10. Matt Miller, *Prison Board Shopping for Inmates to Prevent Lay-Offs*, Patriot-News (Harrisburg, PA), June 22, 1993, at A4.

11. Lindsey Ragas, *Rolling Plains Regional Jail and Detention Center in Haskell Reopens, Creates More Jobs*, KTXS (October 12, 2018).

12. Roxanne Lynne Doty & Elizabeth Shannon Wheatley, *Private Detention and the Immigration Industrial Complex*, 7 Int'l Pol. Soc. 426, 427 (2013).

13. *See* Comer v. Stewart, 215 F.3d 910, 911–12, 918 (9th Cir. 2000); Jana Bommersbach, The Trunk Murderess: Winnie Ruth Judd 2, 45 (1992); Paul Rubin, *Arizona's Worst Criminal*, Phoenix New Times, May 2, 2002, http://www.phoenixnewtimes.com/news/arizonas-worst-criminal-6411416.

14. Roger Mares, *Empty Jail Brings No Jobs to Jones County*, KTXS (May 14, 2012).

15. *See* Franklin E. Zimring & Gordon Hawkins, The Scale of Imprisonment 211 (1993).

16. *See* Gretel Kauffman, *With No ICE Contract, Jerome County Turns to Less Controversial Ways to Fill Its New Jail*, MagicValley.com (December 21, 2017), https://magicvalley.com/news/local/crime-and-courts/with-no-ice-contract -jerome-county-turns-to-less-controversial/article_39c6c42a-6d90-5851-9b11 -176c6ec10a19.html.

17. Associated Press, *Official: Cibola County Facing Prospect of Bankruptcy*, U.S. News & World Report (January 4, 2018, 3:15 PM), https://www.usnews .com/news/best-states/new-mexico/articles/2018-01-04/official-cibola-county -may-be-bankrupt-by-end-of-february.

18. Frederick Melo, *Ramsey County Jail No Longer Taking Immigration Detainees*, Twin Cities Pioneer Press, January 23, 2018, https://www.twincities .com/2018/01/23/ramsey-county-jail-no-longer-taking-immigration-detainees.

19. Stephanie Butts, *ICE Detainees Never Delivered to County*, Waco Tribune-Herald, August 27, 2013, http://www.wacotrib.com/news/mclennan _county/ice-detainees-never-delivered-to-county-s-jail/article_8cefeec0-44d7 -5faa-b323-72c5bc89d65c.html.

20. Jeremy Redmon, *ICE Detention Center Struggling Financially*, Atlanta J.-Const., April 23, 2012, https://www.ajc.com/news/local/ice-detention-center -struggling-financially/tYQJiGzYHNPJEeeM4wY97N/.

21. Fernando del Valle, *Willacy County Braces for Prison Layoffs*, Valley Morning Star, March 6, 2015, http://www.valleymorningstar.com/premium/article _ce6c250c-c484-11e4-b01d-57658f494172.html.

22. Tiffany Huertas, *After Prison Riot, Raymondville Worried About Economic Impact*, ValleyCentral.com (February 24, 2015, 3:40 GMT), http://valley central.com/news/local/after-prison-riot-raymondville-worried-about-economic -impact?id=1168534#.VO6ci8a7JsR.

23. Nat'l Immigrant Justice Ctr., Freedom of Information Act Litigation Reveals Systemic Lack of Accountability in Immigration Detention Contracting 13 (2015).

24. Doty & Wheatley, *supra* note 12, at 427 & note 6.

25. U.S. Dep't of Homeland Security, Immigration & Customs Enforcement, Budget Overview Fiscal Year 2018 Congressional Justification, ICE-O&S-132 (2018).

26. ICE, Performance-Based National Detention Standards 2011, at 407, § 5.8, V(K).

27. U.S. Dep't of Homeland Security, HSCEDM-16-R-00001, Immigration and Customs Enforcement, Performance Work Statement, Florence Detention Center (FDC)—Detention and Transportation Services, at 91 § 8 (2016).

28. Class Action Complaint for Unpaid Wages and Forced Labor, Menocal v. The GEO Group, Inc., No. 1:14-cv-02887, 2014 WL 5389925 (D. Colo. October 22, 2014).

29. Jacqueline Stevens, *One Dollar Per Day: The Slaving Wages of Immigration Jail, From 1943 to Present*, 29 Georg. Immigr. L.J. 391, 396 (2015).

30. Dep't of Homeland Security, Homeland Security Advisory Council, Report of the Subcommittee on Privatized Immigration Detention Facilities 5 (2016).

31. For population and cost amounts, see César Cuauhtémoc García Hernández, *ICE Transitioned from Obama to Trump with Record High Daily Detention Population*, crimmigration.com (April 3, 2018, 12:30 AM), http://crimmigration .com/2018/04/03/ice-transitioned-from-obama-to-trump-with-record-high-daily -detention-population.

32. CoreCivic, 2017 Annual Report Form 10-K 9 (2018).

33. The GEO Group, Inc., 2017 Annual Report 1 (2018).

34. César Cuauhtémoc García Hernández, *If Private Prisons Close . . .* , crimmigration.com (September 1, 2016, 4:00 AM), http://crimmigration.com /2016/09/01/if-private-prisons-close/.

35. Elliot D. Pollack & Company, CCA: Arizona Correctional Facilities Economic and Fiscal Impact Report 2 (2010).

36. Corrections Corp. of America, *New Study Proves Public-Private Partnership in Corrections Energizes State Economies*, PRWeb (February 3, 2010), http://www.prweb.com/releases/arizona_corrections/correctional_facility /prweb3549574.htm; Lauren Millette, *Public Forum on Private Prison Benefits Cancelled*, Prescott eNews (February 9, 2010), https://www.prescottenews.com /index.php/news/current-news/item/14453-public-forum-on-private-prison -benefits-cancelled.

37. Center for Responsive Politics, *For-Profit Prisons*, OpenSecrets.org (last visited November 20, 2018), https://www.opensecrets.org/industries/indus.php ?ind=G7000.

38. Helping Unaccompanied Minors and Alleviating National Emergency Act, H.R. 5114, 113th Cong. (2014).

39. Bob Libal, *Humpday Hall of Shame—Henry Cuellar Wants Kids Deported ASAP, Hauls in Private Prison Cash*, Grassroots Leadership (July 16, 2014), https://grassrootsleadership.org/blog/2014/07/humpday-hall-shame-henry-cuellar -wants-kids-deported-asap-hauls-private-prison-cash.

40. Laura Sullivan, *Prison Economics Help Drive Ariz. Immigration Law*, NPR (October 28, 2010, 11:01 AM), https://www.npr.org/2010/10/28/130833741 /prison-economics-help-drive-ariz-immigration-law.

41. César Cuauhtémoc García Hernández, *Texas Republican Admits He's Pushing Private Prison Corporation's Bill*, crimmigration.com (April 27, 2017, 10:33 AM), http://crimmigration.com/2017/04/27/texas-republican-admits-hes -pushing-private-prison-corporations-bill.

42. *GEO Group Contributions to John N. Raney*, FollowTheMoney.Org (last visited November 20, 2018), https://www.followthemoney.org/show-me?f -eid=6699363&d-eid=1096.

43. CoreCivic, *supra* note 33, at 81; The GEO Group, Inc., *supra* note 34, at 39–40.

44. In the Public Interest, The Banks That Finance Private Prison Companies 3 (2016).

45. CoreCivic, *supra* note 33, at 24, 50.

46. *CoreCivic, Inc. Institutional Ownership*, NASDAQ (November 20, 2018), https://www.nasdaq.com/symbol/cxw/institutional-holdings.

47. *GEO Group Inc (The) Institutional Ownership*, NASDAQ (November 20, 2018), https://www.nasdaq.com/symbol/geo/institutional-holdings.

7: Abolishing Immigration Prisons

1. *Book of Joshua* 6:20 (King James).

2. Doe v. United States, 831 F.3d 309, 320 (5th Cir. 2016); Doe v. Robertson, 751 F.3d 383, 391 (5th Cir. 2014).

3. Angela Y. Davis, Abolition Democracy: Beyond Empire, Prisons, and Torture 75 (2005).

4. Dred Scott v. Sandford, 60 U.S. (19 How.) 393, 407 (1857), *superseded by constitutional amendment*, U.S. Const. amend. XIV.

5. W.E.B. DuBois, The Souls of Black Folk 123 (David W. Blight & Robert Gooding-Williams eds., 1997) (1903).

6. Davis, *supra* note 3, at 111.

7. Michel Foucault, Discipline and Punish: The Birth of the Prison 234 (Alan Sheridan trans., Vintage Books 2d ed. 1995) (1977).

8. U.N. High Comm'r for Refugees, *In Rural Pennsylvania, a Model of Civil Immigration Detention* (January 6, 2011), http://www.refworld.org/docid /4d26cc9c2.html.

9. Charles Dickens, American Notes for General Circulation 51 (1859).

10. Jana K. Lipman, *"The Fish Trusts the Water, and It Is in the Water That It Is Cooked": The Caribbean Origins of the Krome Detention Center*, 2013 Radical Hist. Rev. 115, 123–125 (2013).

11. Carl Lindskoog, Detain and Punish: Haitian Refugees and the Rise of the World's Largest Immigration Detention System 75–76 (2018).

12. *Id.* at 76–79.

13. *Id.* at 73.

14. Michael Flynn, *The Hidden Costs of Human Rights: The Case of Immigration Detention*, 4–5 (Glob. Det. Project, Working Paper No. 7, 2013).

15. Lindskoog, *supra* note 11, at 64.

16. *Id.* at 122–23.

17. Jenna M. Loyd & Alison Mountz, Boats, Borders, and Bases: Race, the Cold War, and the Rise of Migration Detention in the United States 73, 80, 88–89 (2018).

18. Malcolm M. Feeley, *Entrepreneurs of Punishment: The Legacy of Privatization*, 4 Punishment & Soc'y 321, 333 (2002).

19. Mijente, Free Our Future: An Immigration Policy Platform for Beyond the Trump Era 8 (2018).

20. Jennifer Stave et al., Evaluation of the New York Immigrant Family Unity Project: Assessing the Impact of Legal Representation on Family and Community Unity 25 tbl.4, 50, 65 n.64 (2017).

21. *How Often Is The Aggravated Felony Statute Used?*, TRAC Immigration, http://trac.syr.edu/immigration/reports/158/ (last visited November 23, 2018).

22. Shaughnessy v. Mezei, 345 U.S. 206, 224 (1953) (Jackson, J., dissenting).

23. Emily Ryo, *Legal Attitudes of Immigrant Detainees*, 51 Law & Soc'y Rev. 99, 102, 121 (2017).

24. Catholic Legal Immigration Network, Inc., The Needless Detention of Immigrants 27–29 (2000).

25. Megan Golden et al., Vera Institute of Justice, The Appearance Assistance Program: Attaining Compliance with Immigration Laws Through Community Supervision 7 (1998).

26. *Id.* at 14–15.

27. Catholic Legal Immigration Network, Inc., *supra* note 25, at 27.

28. Lutheran Immigration & Refugee Services, Family Placement Alternatives: Promoting Compliance with Compassion and Stability Through Case Management Services 8 (2016).

29. Emily Ryo, *Detained: A Study of Immigration Bond Hearings*, 50 Law & Soc'y Rev. 117, 134 fig.2 (2016).

30. Furman v. Georgia, 408 U.S. 238, 272–73 (1972).

31. Trop v. Dulles, 356 U.S. 86, 100 (1958).

32. Coleman v. Schwarzenegger, 922 F. Supp. 2d 882, 887 (N.D. Cal. 2009).

33. Brown v. Plata, 563 U.S. 493, 510 (2011).

34. Hannah Arendt, The Origins of Totalitarianism 364 (2004).

35. *Id.*

36. Allison Crennen-Dunlap, Comment, *A Constitution That Starves, Beats, and Lashes (Or the Plenary Power Doctrine):* Jennings v. Rodriguez *and a Peek into Immigration Dissent History*, 95 Denver L. Rev. 95, 103 (2018).

37. Saskia Sassen, Guests and Aliens 155–56 (1999).

38. Chancellery of El Salvador, *El Cuento de Coyote*, YouTube (July 15, 2014), https://www.youtube.com/watch?v=Uu8d62Xe7rk.

39. Ron Nixon, *U.S. Campaign Against Migration Goes Unheard, or Unheeded, in Guatemala*, New York Times, October 7, 2018, https://www.nytimes.com/2018/10/07/world/americas/guatemala-immigration-usa-mexico-border.html.

40. Jennifer M. Chacón, *Overcriminalizing Migration*, 102 J. Crim. L. & Criminology 613, 649 n.186 (2012).

41. *See* Comm. on Law & Justice, Nat'l Research Council, Budgeting for Immigration Enforcement: A Path to Better Performance 34–35 (Steve Redburn et al. eds., 2011); Marc. R. Rosenblum, Unaccompanied Child Migration to the United States: The Tension Between Protection and Prevention 19 (2015); Wayne A. Cornelius & Idean Salehyan, *Does Border Enforcement Deter Unauthorized Immigration? The Case of Mexican Migration to the United States*, 1 Reg. & Governance 139, 145 (2007).

42. Jacob I. Stowell et al., *Latino Crime and Latinos in the Criminal Justice System: Trends, Policy Implications, and Future Research Initiatives*, 4 Race & Soc. Problems 31, 36 (2012).

43. Robert Adelman et al., *Urban Crime Rates and the Changing Face of Immigration: Evidence Across Four Decades*, 15 J. Ethnicity in Crim. Just. 52, 70 (2017).

44. Matthew T. Lee & Ramiro Martinez, Jr., *Immigration and Asian Homicide Patterns in Urban and Suburban San Diego, in* Immigration and Crime:

Race, Ethnicity, and Violence 90, 109 (Ramiro Martinez, Jr. & Abel Valenzuela, Jr., eds., 2006); Jeffrey D. Morenhoff & Avraham Astor, *Immigrant Assimilation and Crime: Generational Differences in Youth Violence in Chicago, in* Immigration and Crime: Race, Ethnicity, and Violence 36, 55–56 (Ramiro Martinez, Jr. & Abel Valenzuela, Jr., eds., 2006); Amie L. Nielsen & Ramiro Martinez, Jr., *Multiple Disadvantages and Crime Among Black Immigrants: Exploring Haitian Violence in Miami's Communities, in* Immigration and Crime: Race, Ethnicity, and Violence 212, 227–28 (Ramiro Martinez, Jr. & Abel Valenzuela, Jr., eds., 2006).

45. Jennifer L. Truman & Rachel E. Morgan, *Criminal Victimization*, Bureau of Just. Stat. 1, 5 (2016).

46. United States v. Goodwin, 457 U.S. 368, 382 (1982).

47. In re Davis, 130 S. Ct. 1, 3 (2009) (Scalia, J., dissenting).

48. Missouri v. Frye, 566 U.S. 134, 144 (quoting Robert E. Scott & William J. Stuntz, *Plea Bargaining as Contract*, 101 Yale L.J. 1909, 1912 (1992)).

49. Kate Kelly & David Enrich, *Kavanaugh's Yearbook Is "Horrible, Hurtful" to a Woman It Named*, New York Times, September 24, 2018, https://www.nytimes.com/2018/09/24/business/brett-kavanaugh-yearbook-renate.html.

50. Matter of Valenzuela Gallardo, 27 I&N Dec. 449, 461 (2018).

Conclusion

1. Slavoj Žižek, *Terrorists with a Human Face, in* The Final Countdown: Europe, Refugees and the Left, 187, 199 (Jela Krečič ed., 2017).

2. Thomas Nail, The Figure of the Migrant 1 (2015).

ABOUT THE AUTHOR

César Cuauhtémoc García Hernández is a professor of law at the University of Denver and an immigration lawyer. He runs the blog *Crimmigration.com* and regularly speaks on immigration law and policy issues. He has appeared in the *New York Times*, the *Wall Street Journal*, NPR, *The Guardian*, and many other venues.

PUBLISHING IN THE PUBLIC INTEREST

Thank you for reading this book published by The New Press. The New Press is a nonprofit, public interest publisher. New Press books and authors play a crucial role in sparking conversations about the key political and social issues of our day.

We hope you enjoyed this book and that you will stay in touch with The New Press. Here are a few ways to stay up to date with our books, events, and the issues we cover:

- Sign up at www.thenewpress.com/subscribe to receive updates on New Press authors and issues and to be notified about local events
- Like us on Facebook: www.facebook.com/newpress books
- Follow us on Twitter: www.twitter.com/thenewpress

Please consider buying New Press books for yourself; for friends and family; or to donate to schools, libraries, community centers, prison libraries, and other organizations involved with the issues our authors write about.

The New Press is a 501(c)(3) nonprofit organization. You can also support our work with a tax-deductible gift by visiting www.thenewpress.com/donate.